Rethinking Small-group Instruction
in the Intermediate Grades

Differentiation That Makes a Difference

Nancy N. Boyles

Maupin House

Rethinking Small-group Instruction in the Intermediate Grades
Differentiation That Makes a Difference

By Nancy N. Boyles

Cover design: Studio Montage
Book design: Mickey Cuthbertson

Library of Congress Cataloging-in-Publication Data

Boyles, Nancy N., 1948-
 Rethinking small-group instruction in the intermediate grades :
differentiation that makes a difference / by Nancy N. Boyles.
     p. cm.
 Includes bibliographical references.
 ISBN 978-1-934338-86-5 (pbk.)
1. Reading (Middle school) 2. Guided reading. 3. Group work in
education. I. Title.
 LB1632.B694 2010
 428.4071'2--dc22
                          2010038839

Also by Nancy Boyles

Teaching Written Response to Text: Constructing Quality Answers to Open-Ended Comprehension Questions

Constructing Meaning through Kid-Friendly Comprehension Strategy Instruction

Hands-On Literacy Coaching

That's a GREAT Answer! Teaching Literature Response to K-3, ELL, and Struggling Readers

Launching RTI Comprehension Instruction with Shared Reading: 40 Model Lessons for Intermediate Readers

Maupin House publishes professional resources for K-12 educators. Contact us for tailored, in-school training or to schedule an author for a workshop or conference. Visit www.maupinhouse.com for free lesson plan downloads.

Maupin House Publishing, Inc.

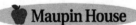

2416 NW 71 Place
Gainesville, FL 32653
www.maupinhouse.com
800-524-0634
352-373-5588
352-373-5546 (fax)
info@maupinhouse.com

10 9 8 7 6 5 4 3 2 1

Dedication
Dedicated to…the Red Robe

You are reading this book today because of a red robe long ago. And that's not even much of a stretch. I was perched with the rest of the choir on the steps of Thomsom Hall at Wilson College, the small women's college I attended in bucolic southern Pennsylvania. It was my sophomore year and the opening convocation was about to begin under the warm sun of an early September sky. This was a great vantage point from which to view the parade of faculty decked out in their academic regalia, winding their way along the cobblestoned path from the chapel to the school's main academic building.

"Who's that?" I whispered to my friend Nan standing in the row in front of mine. She didn't know. What caught my eye was not some cute, young male faculty member, but the robe this man was wearing. It was red. It alone stood out among the sea of somber black gowns in which most of the other professors were clad. "I want one of those," I announced to no one in particular.

It turned out that the wearer of the red robe was the new education prof. (There were two in the whole department.) "So where did you get that robe?" I asked at the end of my first-ever education class. "Dr. Red Robe" was more than happy to tell me about his newly-minted Ed.D. from Boston University. Red was the color signifying the university from which the degree had been granted.

I wish I could say that the education courses I took in my undergraduate years were life changing, the kind of cutting-edge stuff that guarantees a newbie teacher will hit the ground running when she accepts her first teaching position. Well, no, that wasn't quite the case for me way back then. I have one particularly pathetic memory of a textbook for the only course required at the time for math and reading methods. Imagine: A total of three credits for everything a new teacher would need to know to teach reading *and* math! Here's the part I remember most vividly: The front half of that textbook was titled *Math Methods*. And if you flipped it over and upside down, a different title proclaimed *Reading Methods*. I have no memory of what actually lay between those two covers—or if I even read that book. But if my skill was lacking in the little country school where I eventually student taught, my enthusiasm for my almost-teacher role must have compensated.

While the pedagogy may not have been life changing, I had found a mentor in "Dr. Red Robe," whose wisdom casually dispersed along the way had a longer-ranging impact: "If you love this teaching business as much as I think you do, you're not going to be happy until you have a doctoral diploma hanging on your wall." Neither of us could have predicted then how that counsel would shape the decades to come.

And then, for reasons that really were deeper than the color of the robe (honest!), I did choose Boston University for my graduate studies—first for a master's degree, then a sixth-year certificate, and finally an Ed.D.—a doctorate of education. I was now the proud wearer of my very own red robe, complete with wide bands of black velvet circling the long bell sleeves and a hood so regal that I feel compelled to act quite grownup and proper when wearing it.

Fast forward more than 30 years, an entire career: Twenty-five grand years as a classroom teacher and currently another ten years-plus teaching graduate students (practicing teachers) in a university program that certifies reading consultants—and traveling the country talking to you and you and you. While the literacy pedagogy I share may or may not resonate with you as "life changing," I hope at the very least it inspires you to rethink your current practice and reaffirm or readjust.

Indeed my red robe has taken me places I never dreamed I would go. I have only one regret. A few years ago, I read in my college *Alumnae Quarterly* that "Dr. Red Robe" had passed away. I wished somewhere along the way I had thought to say thank you. And although it wasn't the same as telling the man himself, I was able to locate his widow and shared the story of the red robe with her.

The legacy of that red robe lives on. It's not hard to pick me out of a faculty lineup at a commencement ceremony or convocation. "Where'd you get that robe?" students always ask me. Of course I tell them. But I hope I tell them other helpful things, too, from time to time, mentoring them as educators and future leaders as I was once mentored. *This is someone's child*, I often remind myself as I sit with a student (ages 22 to grandma) to plan a program, confer about a certification—or whatever. *Someone's mother would want me to offer up this extra measure of challenge or support or kindness.* The trick is…figuring out for each one of them exactly what the most powerful challenge or support or kindness might be—sometimes even before they see it themselves. That is the real legacy of the red robe—and the reason this book is dedicated to it—from mentee to mentor and the journey we take between.

Table of Contents

Part I

UNDERSTANDING SMALL-GROUP INSTRUCTION IN THE INTERMEDIATE GRADES

CHAPTER ONE
What's Up with Small-group Instruction in the Intermediate Grades? Issues and Concerns

CHAPTER TWO
Making Sense of Differentiation

CHAPTER THREE
Frequently Asked Questions about Small-group Instruction......... 33

Part II
IMPLEMENTING SMALL-GROUP INSTRUCTION: A MENU OF POSSIBILITIES 39

INTRODUCTION TO PART II...41

CHAPTER FOUR
Constructing Basic Meaning: The Prequel...............................49

Files on the CD

CHAPTER FIVE
Reinforcing Comprehension Skills and Strategies

Comprehension Standards and Objectives
Instructional Map for an Explicit Standards-based RTI Tier 1 Comprehension Lesson
Target Template
Rubric for Assessing Students' Oral and Written Response to Comprehension Questions
Written-response Check Sheet
Strategy Points for Focus Lessons
Instructional Map for an Explicit Strategy Lesson
Rubric for Using Individual Strategies Accurately and Insightfully
Checklist for Using Individual Comprehension Strategies
Possible Fluency Focus Lessons
Poems for Fluency Focus Lessons
Fluency Rubric
Fluency Checklist
Template for Vocabulary Connections or Vocabulary Pyramid: Words in Context
Template for Vocabulary Connections: Student Activity
Model for Vocabulary Connections: Student Activity
Template for Vocabulary Pyramid 1
Template for Vocabulary Pyramid 2
Model for Vocabulary Pyramid: Vocabulary in Context
Model Vocabulary Pyramid
Target Sheets Matched to Each Objective
Rubric for Assessing Vocabulary Knowledge and Use
Vocabulary Checklist
Author's Craft: Find It in a Book
Monitoring My Thinking about Writing Traits When I Read
Author's Crafts to Find in My Reading
How to Explain Writing Traits to Students
Rubric for Assessing a Student's Understanding of Author's Crafts
Checklist for Author's Crafts

CHAPTER SIX
Extending Literacy Learning Through Discussion

Ways to Have a Good Discussion
Literature Discussion Prompts
Rubric for Examining Teachers' Expertise in Leading a Discussion
Discussion Rubric for Assessing Student Discourse
Checklist for Reflecting on Discussion Skills
Discussion Planner for A-D Strand Comprehension Questions
Discussion Questions for Deep Thinking about Comprehension Strategies
Discussion Planner for Comprehension Strategies
Thinking Outside the Box Template with Suggested Generic Questions
Thinking Outside the Box Template
Thinking Outside the Box Mini-Posters

CHAPTER SEVEN
When They "Can't Read"—Teaching Primary Skills in the Intermediate Grades

Introduction

WHAT? ANOTHER BOOK?

It was a cold, gray day in February, and my husband and I were at the Cape for the weekend. Most people think of Cape Cod as a summer destination—sand between the toes, lobster, family fun. But we love it year round. Picture a funky little beach house a stone's throw from the bay (our "someplace else"), doggie curled up in front of the fire, husband in the kitchen whipping up a hefty pot of clam chowder, and me…at my computer. (Well, some things never change, regardless of the location.)

I had been sitting there for an hour plotting a workshop I'd agreed to present for a district on small-group instruction a couple of weeks hence.

> Ron (a.k.a. Mr. Nancy Boyles): What are you doing?
> Nancy: Writing a book.

The clattering pans in the kitchen stopped clattering.

> Ron: You just finished a book. You said you were done with books for a while.
> Nancy: I changed my mind.

In fact, I'd had no intention of starting another book right now and was as surprised as Ron when those words fell from my lips. But it was true; I *had* to write this book. As I sorted through documents filed away on my laptop under "small-group instruction," I suddenly saw a structure that would make small-group instruction make sense to intermediate-grade teachers.

We struggle so much with the whole concept of small-group instruction, especially beyond the primary grades. And how do we *differentiate* that small-group instruction? The pattern that emerged for me was not one I'd seen described anywhere else, and I felt an urgent need to write it all right now.

> Nancy: If I could just stay here for the week, I think I could get most of this manuscript done.

No comment from the kitchen, but Ron was probably seeing the next few months of his life flash before his eyes; he's been down this road a few times before—shoving sandwiches under the door as I scramble like a mad woman to layer a book project on top of teaching my classes and school visits and conferences and all those meetings that we educators face endlessly.

This truly was an opportunity to *rethink* small-group instruction—in the context of so many things that I've thought about and written about over the last decade:

- Comprehension strategies: How do they fit into the mix for small-group instruction?

- Specific comprehension objectives aligned with high-stakes standards: Where do they fit?

- Literacy components that contribute to comprehension, such as fluency and vocabulary and author's craft: Is there a place for them in our small-group teaching, too?

- Discussion (which has somehow taken a back seat to our highly focused instruction): Can we bring that back in a meaningful way while also teaching explicitly?

- And what about our intermediate-grade students who continue to function at a primary level? What can we do for them in our small groups?

WHAT THIS BOOK IS ABOUT—AND WHY YOU WILL WANT TO READ IT

I've answered all of these questions and more in this book, offering sixteen different options for small-group instruction for students who need to: construct basic meaning about a text, reinforce particular comprehension skills and strategies, and learn the art of discourse leading to higher-level critical and creative thinking. I've included all of the resources you'll need to implement these instructional formats, too—rubrics and checklists, planning templates, prompts, and so much more.

This material is intended mostly for classroom teachers of the intermediate grades—anywhere from third grade through middle school. Even second-grade teachers may find this book useful for students fluent at that grade level. I also hope literacy coaches will share these instructional techniques with teachers in their building. And I hope administrators will look for teaching rich with the many learning opportunities that this book suggests as they visit classrooms and help teachers reflect on their practice.

Small-group instruction is too often the missing piece in RTI where the classroom teacher is responsible for meeting the needs of *all* students at the tier 1 level. Find answers in this book to differentiate that instruction so it will make the needed difference for students. Find out, too, how to embed the Common Core State Standards into your small-group instruction and how these standards can make your teaching even more powerful.

HOW THIS BOOK IS ORGANIZED

This book is divided into two parts. **Part I: Understanding Small-group Instruction in the Intermediate Grades** contains three short chapters to set the stage for the instructional formats that follow:

- **Chapter One: What's Up with Small-group Instruction in the Intermediate Grades? Issues and Concerns.** This illuminates a number of dilemmas common to small-group instruction at the intermediate grade level.

- **Chapter Two: Making Sense of Differentiation.** Learn what it means to differentiate the literacy process, product, and content for students reading at different levels with different literacy needs.

- **Chapter Three: Frequently Asked Questions about Small-group Instruction.** The questions answered in this chapter relate to the "how-to" of getting small-group instruction off the ground in your classroom.

Part II: Implementing Small-group Instruction: A Menu of Possibilities contains all sixteen of the formats divided into four mega-chapters. Before exploring them, though, be sure to check out the "Introduction to Part II," which includes a really streamlined *Small-group Planner* and an extensive annotated bibliography of authentic short texts useful for small-group instruction in the intermediate grades and middle school.

- **Chapter Four: Constructing Basic Meaning: The Prequel.** Included in this chapter are five instructional formats to help students achieve a basic level of understanding about what they read. Comprehension for both literary and informational reading is addressed through comprehension strategies and text elements.

- **Chapter Five: Reinforcing Skills and Strategies.** Reinforce important literacy standards through the five formats targeted in this chapter that focus not just on comprehension strategies and standards-based objectives, but also on vocabulary, fluency, and author's craft.

- **Chapter Six: Extending Literacy Learning through Discussion.** Teach students five different formats for talking about text—literary and informational—to generate both critical and creative thinking.

- **Chapter Seven: When They "Can't Read"—Teaching Primary Skills in the Intermediate Grades.** If students (at any grade level) are still "getting to fluency," the instruction needs to be different than that which we offer students whose main focus is comprehension. In this chapter, learn exactly how to meet the needs of your most struggling students within their small group.

This book also contains a **CD** with all of the reproducibles included—an important perk for busy teachers whose time is so valuable—as well as target sheets matched to each objective that explain how to find the best evidence to meet the objective. Look for this icon ( ) throughout the book, indicating what files are available on the CD.

THE CHAPTER I NEVER WROTE

As I pondered the possibility of this book on that dreary February day, I envisioned a final chapter about independent reading. After all, I had written about shared reading (*Launching RTI Comprehension Instruction with Shared Reading: 40 Lessons for Intermediate Readers*, Maupin House, 2009). And now this book was to feature small-group instruction. How could I *not* complete the symphony by attending to this other critical component of the literacy curriculum?

Then I started writing, mostly at home in Connecticut and after my semester ended at the Cape, for as many stolen days as I could manage. The pages just kept coming…and coming…and coming. I realized it was unrealistic to think that I could embark on a whole new focus at the very end of what had already become very comprehensive in scope.

It worries me a little that this chapter is not included because I would not want anyone to conclude—just because I haven't written about it—that I don't value independent reading. Independent reading is the glue that holds literacy learning together. We have shared reading to introduce concepts, small-group instruction to reinforce them, and independent reading to practice what has been learned in a way that builds stamina and enjoyment. If we want children to *choose* to read, we need to give them opportunities to do so. But that, as I said, will need to be a conversation for a different day.

Enjoy the reading ahead. Oh, and in case you were wondering, the clam chowder was DELICIOUS!

Part I:

Understanding Small-group Instruction in the Intermediate Grades

Chapter One

What's Up with Small-group Instruction in the Intermediate Grades? Issues and Concerns

THE VIEW FROM YESTERDAY

When I was a kid in elementary school, we had "reading groups." (We also had Dick, Jane, and Sally—who some of you might remember if your educational past dates back as many decades as my own.) The thing about those reading groups was that they never changed: Once a Bluebird, always a Bluebird. And for the most part, I'm not talking about a full year of being a Bluebird; I'm talking about your entire elementary school career. One's whole reputation could ride on which reading group you were in, or so it seemed to me. This explains why half a century later I still vividly remember the day my third-grade teacher called me to the reading table with the middle reading group. The *middle* group? What was going on here? I was a good reader. I had been in the *high* group since I opened that first little pre-primer in first grade. Complete meltdown! Locked myself in the bathroom when I got home and refused to come out until Mom promised to get to the bottom of this. (I wish I could say I was making this up.) I don't remember how the situation got resolved, but since I did ultimately finish third grade and went on to live a more or less productive life without too many emotional scars, I'm guessing I was swiftly returned to my "rightful" place in the group with all the best readers.

Apparently, I wasn't the only kid out there with "Reading Group Syndrome" because a generation or so later, someone had the bright idea of doing away with homogeneous reading groups, perhaps for the psychological damage they could cause. During the whole-language heyday there were basically *no* reading groups in some classrooms. The approach then was to get kids excited about books, let them loose to choose the books they would read, and confer with them individually as time allowed. The problem was that time didn't allow for all that much conferring when there was one teacher in the classroom and twenty-five students. And when the teacher hadn't read most of the books, well, that wasn't exactly conducive to meaningful teacher guidance either. Out with Dick, Jane, and Sally (and their cronies inside the covers of basals by other publishers). Welcome, anthologies—the precursors of today's mega-core programs. True to the whole-language tradition, these weighty tomes offered our youngest readers "authentic literature," stories that contained natural-sounding language very different from the repetitive patterns uttered by Dick and Jane: "*Look, Dick, look. See Spot. See Spot run. Run, Spot, run.*" Because there was so much to "cover" in these programs, instruction stayed mostly at the whole-class level. The idea was that if students just read the story over and over (or listened to it on tape), the words—and the meaning—would magically sink in. Meanwhile, in the intermediate grades, teachers were instructed to move from whole-class instruction to "small, flexible groups." Except lots of teachers never quite got the hang of flexible grouping. Although NCLB (No Child Left Behind) had yet to arrive on the scene, most states were beginning to implement some form of annual high-stakes testing. The results were not pretty. Could students' poor comprehension be the result of teaching that didn't really meet their developmental needs?

The response? Guided reading. This instructional format was designed especially for young children as a means of helping them integrate all of the components of fluent reading. In guided reading, students are grouped by level based on assessment data. Assessments are administered regularly and children are regrouped as their levels change. Instead of reading from a hefty anthology, there are little leveled books. Instead of a predetermined scope and sequence, teachers are directed to address in-the-moment needs that students demonstrate as they are reading. At least that's the plan. In reality, many teachers have difficulty truly *teaching* to students' needs. They pull together small groups of children reading at DRA level 6 or 14 or 20. But beyond practicing reading at a particular level, many teachers are unclear about exactly what they should be doing to help students move forward.

When skillful teachers implement guided reading in the primary grades, this model can be effective. Unfortunately, "traditional" guided reading is not as effective once students achieve fluency at approximately the second-grade level, when attention rightfully turns to comprehension. Furthermore, at more advanced reading levels, the lines become blurred with regard to text leveling as background knowledge and interest are factored into what students can and will read.

If not guided reading in the intermediate grades, then what? Lots of classroom teachers beyond the primary grades still have an affinity for those duplicated packets containing long lists of comprehension questions and vocabulary words. While these pages do, to some extent, *test* reading, they do not *teach* reading. The tradition here is so long that I doubt any of us can remember a time when reading was not "taught" this way. More significantly, the "tradition" is still very much alive in too many of today's classrooms.

THE VIEW FROM TODAY

In my frequent visits to classrooms, generally grades two through six, the prevailing small-group winds seem to blow in two directions. Either teachers are stuck in "junior-high mode," assigning and assessing as they might have done in the 1960s. Or, the teaching looks very primary with kids in bigger bodies doing the sorts of guided-reading things that may work well in kindergarten and first grade when children are getting to fluency—but that don't pack much punch for more competent readers when the concern is comprehension.
Come with me on a couple of virtual visits to intermediate-grade classrooms where teachers are working with their small groups. As you "watch" these teachers, consider:

- How would you rate this lesson? Why?

- Did the teacher use instructional strategies with a strong research base?

- What did the children learn in their small-group session today?

- How would you have instructed the group? (Think about engagement, lesson focus, instructional practices, and follow up.)

MR. FORD'S FIFTH GRADE

Mr. Ford (fifth-grade teacher) dismissed the "Rockets" back to their seats and called his top group. Six "Eagles" scurried to the table, where they quickly opened their reading folders and pulled out stapled packets of questions and other activities related to the novel they were reading: *Holes* by Louis Sachar. Today's assignment was to complete the vocabulary and questions for chapters three and four on pages 6-15 of the book:

1. *Why did Stanley have a box of stationery?*

2. *How do we know that Stanley was very unhappy at home?*

3. *How did Mrs. Bell inadvertently embarrass Stanley?*

4. *Briefly explain the curse of the one-legged Gypsy.*

5. *Why did Stanley's apartment smell of burning rubber and foot odor?*

6. *What did everyone in the family like about Stanley Yelnat's name?*

7. *Explain the abundance of sunflower seeds on the floor by the desk.*

8. *How did the guard wish to be addressed by Stanley?*

9. *Explain how the laundry was done.*

10. *What instructions did the guard give to Stanley concerning digging?*

11. *According to Mr. Sir why did none of the campers attempt to escape despite the fact that there were no fences or guard towers?*

Vocabulary: *stationery, obstacle, ratios, convicted, gypsy, curse, descendants, perseverance, neglected, barren, desolate, violation, premises*

Mr. Ford glanced around the table and was pleased that everyone had completed all of the questions. He called on Maria first. "Read us the definition you found for *stationery*." She turned her paper over and read the words she'd copied from the dictionary.

"Jack, tell us the sentence you wrote with that word." Jack read his sentence, which, though short, demonstrated the correct meaning of this homophone. Mr. Ford then mentioned to students the other *stationary*, pointing out the different spelling and its definition. The same sequence prevailed for the remaining twelve words: definition, sentence that incorporated the word, and teacher clarification if necessary. Sara and Ebony doodled on their worksheet, one eye to the vocabulary task, making elaborate "correct" marks next to each word.

"Don't forget to hand in your definitions and sentences before going back to your seats," Mr. Ford reminded everyone. Sara and Ebony were still doodling; the rest of the Eagles nodded mechanically, flipping in unison to the beginning of chapter three. Mike B. slouched in his chair which won him the honor of reading first. Mike B. was a good oral reader and didn't miss a beat as he flew from one line to the next. Sara took a break from her now exquisitely decorated vocabulary paper to estimate when it would be her turn. She counted the kids to the left of Mike B. (three). She counted forward three pages. *Probably page ten,* she concluded. *Perfect, a short one.* (Sara wasn't a smooth oral reader and always worried that she'd stumble over some stupid word and hear about it later from Mike B. or Raymond.

The group whipped through the rest of chapter three and even chapter four. "We're out of time," Mr. Ford announced as children began to pull out their question packets. "Just hand in your questions and I'll correct them myself. Your assignment is to read the next two chapters, do the vocabulary, and answer the questions. If you don't finish before lunch, take your packet home, but don't forget to bring it back tomorrow. The Eagles packed up and headed back to their seats as swiftly as they had arrived. The next time Mr. Ford glanced around the room, *Holes* was propped open on everyone's desk.

So what do you think? Hopefully, you were not impressed. On a scale of one to ten, you might have given Mr. Ford about a *two*. (I guess we do have to give him at least a little credit for even working with small groups—unlike some intermediate-grade teachers who only provide whole-class instruction.) Still, Mr. Ford doesn't appear to have gotten the memo about a few practices that just don't have a solid research base:

- Long lists of questions, mostly at the literal thinking level (there were eleven here—for a mere nine pages of text)
- Looking up definitions in a dictionary (no research support for this for a variety of reasons, not the least of which is that the target word is often defined using other words that students don't understand)
- Round-robin reading (promotes low level of engagement and embarrasses readers who lack fluency)

What did these students learn today? That would be difficult to determine because there didn't seem to be any particular objective. The focus, such as it was, was on the *reading* (the content of the text) rather than the *reader* (what it takes to build the kinds of strategies that help us to engage with text more meaningfully).

You may have easily reached the same conclusions about Mr. Ford's lesson that I did; as educators, we're quite adept at zeroing in on *problems*. But how would you have taught this small group? Answering that question gives us pause. Let's hold that thought for the moment—until we consider our options. It's not that any one of us couldn't improve on Mr. Ford's lesson right now. But a more thorough understanding of the possibilities for meeting small-group needs await us in Part II of this book and will empower us to deliver the kind of small-group teaching that in turn empowers our students. First, let's peek in on one more classroom, this time a third grade, where Ms. Babbit has just called the "Red" group to the kidney-shaped table in the back of the room. How would you rate Ms. Babbit's teaching, and how does it measure up against standards of high-quality instruction?

MS. BABBIT'S THIRD GRADE

As students slid into their chairs, Ms. Babbit pulled out a new book, *Princess Petunia and the Case of the Lost Jewels*. The number scrawled on the back of the text was "34," a perfect match for three of the five students in the book, according to their most recent DRA testing. Josh was technically a "30" and Carlos was closer to a "38," but he had some language issues and Ms. Babbit thought he'd do better here than with the next highest group (all strong "40s.")

"I read this before," Josh announced before his teacher even had a chance to pass out the books." "I read it last year when I was in third grade." Ms. Babbit groaned silently. Josh was a repeater, but he wasn't anywhere close to level 34 last year; how could he have read this book already?

"That's okay," Ms. Babbit replied. "Sometimes it's fun to read a book a second time. You can learn even more about it." Now she distributed the books and asked everyone to look at the cover and the title. "What do you think the story will be about?"

Luis: "A princess. And some jewels. The jewels are in a case."

Josh: "No, Luis. It's not that kind of case, not like a box. See the magnifying glass?" *Case* means it's like a mystery. The princess is holding a magnifying glass. You have to solve the mystery, but I already know…"

Ms. Babbit quickly interceded before Josh gave away the entire plot. The group generally did a picture walk before beginning a text. However, this book was comprised of little chapters, so picture clues were in short supply. "Read chapter one silently," she instructed, "and look for what's important. Today I'll lean in and listen to Carlos read in a 'whisper voice.'"

Everyone did as they were told. Josh zipped through all three pages of the chapter and spent the remaining time trying to balance his pencil on his eraser as he waited for the others to finish. Luis and Vanessa were sitting on either side of Carlos, whose "whisper voice" was considerably more than a "whisper" and distracted them from their own reading. Carlos read smoothly, though he had no idea how to respond when his teacher questioned him about some of the jewels mentioned in the text: *diamonds, emeralds, rubies*. They all had to wait for Anna to finish; in fact, she may not have even read the final page completely.

"So what was important in chapter one?" Ms. Babbit asked. A couple of students got busy thumbing through the three pages they'd read; the others just looked blank. Silence. More silence. "Well, I thought it was important that Princess Petunia looked in her jewelry box and her diamond necklace was missing. What else was missing?" Still more silence.

Ms. Babbit sighed. "I think you should go back to your seats and reread these pages. Then I want you to write two things you learned in this chapter that you think were important." Josh was poised to respond with his favorite line—*I don't get it*—when the bell rang and everyone scurried back to their seats to line up for lunch.

It looks like Ms. Babbit has attended the workshop on guided reading and has taken good notes. She's using appropriate leveled texts. There's reference to the characteristic picture walk, and students engage in "whisper reading," with the teacher listening in. There is a lesson focus (*Look for what's important*). But, this just didn't work out. After reading the designated pages, no student could, in fact, identify what was important. What happened here? Without any verification of comprehension, it would be difficult to rate this lesson as any more successful than the one delivered by Mr. Ford. What's unsettling here, however, is that you could make the case that Ms. Babbit *was* using research-based practices.

The way I see it, Ms. Babbit is just going through the motions. She's following the instructional protocol she's learned, and when it doesn't produce the intended results, well… that's the kids' fault. (Big sigh: *"I think you should go back to your seats and reread these pages."*) That's the back-up plan? Without more than "rereading these pages," it's hard to envision these students returning to this table tomorrow with the important points of their story neatly outlined.

Truth to tell, this plan was destined for an unhappy ending from the start. The instructional model featured here—which we know as *guided reading* and which does work quite well with emergent and beginning readers blessed with knowledgeable teachers who recognize a teachable moment when they see one and instantaneously teach to that need—doesn't work nearly as well when the instructional focus is comprehension rather than word-level skills and fluency.

PREVALENT PROBLEMS WITH SMALL-GROUP INSTRUCTION

The scenarios above describe two prevalent problems with small-group instruction in the intermediate grades—but there are more. The following list identifies seven fairly common problems that I have witnessed in classrooms

1. **It is mostly "assign and assess."** The mantra here is "Answer these questions, come back tomorrow, and we will correct them." There is no real focus to the group session other than the content of the reading, often a chapter in a chapter book. This small-group format tends to include hefty packets of questions (lots of them at a literal level), which may take weeks to complete.

2. **It mimics guided reading in the primary grades.** The session may begin with a picture walk (if there are pictures in the text). Most of the group time is spent "whisper reading" with the teacher listening in on individual students to check their fluency. Students are grouped by level, but there is little effort to address their specific reading needs as determined by various assessments. Students mostly just *practice* reading.

3. **It happens only occasionally.** In some classrooms, small-group instruction is not a consistent part of students' literacy work; the teacher meets with each group only once or twice per week. The teacher (and students) may not even know who is in which group, and/or there may be so many groups that it is nearly impossible to meet with them regularly.

4. **It doesn't happen at all—reason #1.** Reading in some intermediate classrooms continues to be all about the anthology from the core program or the whole-class novel, both of which consume the entire literacy block with no time remaining for meeting with small groups. (This is often intentional on the part of the teacher with claims of "too much to cover" to meet with small groups.)

5. **It doesn't happen at all—reason #2.** In a classroom where reader's workshop is the instructional model, students may all read different books, with the teacher conferring with them individually. This can work if the teacher has read all of the books her students read and is masterful at instantly identifying a reader's needs—as well as getting to all students as often as necessary. Otherwise, conferring is both inefficient and ineffective and provides too little time for students to talk about their reading with each other.

6. **It happens, but a student leads the group.** The students come to the group and the teacher asks, "Who would like to be the leader today?" A few hands shoot up; other students want no part of this. The teacher hands the leader for the day a sheet of prompts and the text, which no one has read at this point. "Does anyone have any predictions?" the leader inquires. "Now read to see if you need anything clarified or if you have any questions…" "Can someone summarize this?" We would never encourage a teacher to "wing it" with no planning prior to meeting with a small group—but this is exactly what happens when we suddenly drop a child into this teacher role. The intent here is to give students more voice within the small-group experience. But lots of times, the leader doesn't even understand the text himself. How effective is his leadership destined to be? And reading a sequence of prescribed prompts off a cue card hardly generates great discussion.

7. **It happens, but the teacher isn't present.** In many intermediate classrooms, students get together in book clubs or literature circles without their teacher present to talk about books they have read. As long as they are competent comprehension-strategy users and committed to the task at hand, these groups are a great way for students to practice the skills they have already learned. Recognize, however, that this is actually a means of *independent* reading; small-group *instruction* calls for a teacher to be involved to help students learn and reinforce reading strategies they are just developing.

Without better small-group options, it's no wonder that some teachers are so willing to abort the mission and just teach the whole-class novel. But we shouldn't abandon small-group work. We want students to have the opportunity to read in small groups for two reasons. First, we need to meet their developmental needs—which we can't do when the entire class reads the same book. Any book that the whole class reads together will be too easy for some students and too difficult for others. We need to teach to students' *instructional* level, using text with *some* challenge to stretch their thinking, but not so much challenge that they will become discouraged and give up. We now have plenty of assessment data so that we can move kids around when we see that their needs have changed; their placement in a group is no longer a life sentence. The other reason we want students to work in small groups is for the opportunities for interaction that small groups provide. With five or six children sitting around a table, *everyone* can interact, and the teacher can monitor each student's progress much more thoroughly.

But what exactly will students *do* around that small table? By the time students get into the intermediate grades (probably grade three, but possibly grade two for high-performing students and even the end of first grade for our most competent readers), their time in small groups can be spent in many different ways. While the intent of our work in small groups is to *guide* readers, I propose that we use a different label than *guided reading* to describe this work. *Guided reading* congers up a particular image; the ways that we will work with students in small groups in the intermediate grades are not consistent with what we see in our minds when we use this term. Let's just call this *small-group instruction*. The only territory we're claiming here is size (small!) and intent (instruction—meaning a teacher is involved).

Sitting with a few students around a table (or cross-legged on the floor on carpet squares or outside under the shade of a tall tree), we can structure students' literacy learning in so many different ways. The format and focus of our small-group instruction will vary according to the varied needs of our students. Because our students have different needs, we must teach them differently. This is differentiation. This is what the remainder of this book describes: the many ways small-group instruction can take shape in the intermediate grades.

MOVING FORWARD

Part II of this book will provide you with the *how* of differentiation: How do we differentiate our small-group reading instruction to meet the needs of *all* of our students? More basic than this question, however, is the *what* of differentiation? *What* do we really mean by *differentiation*? *What* do we differentiate in our small-group reading instruction? Chapter Two answers these questions. But first, take some time to reflect on the issues and concerns raised in Chapter One.

QUESTIONS TO CONSIDER

1. When you were a student in the intermediate grades, was there small-group instruction in your class? What was it like? Try to recollect some of the details and share them with your colleagues.

2. Do you struggle with any of the same issues as those described in this chapter? Which ones? In what ways are they a concern or problem to you?

3. Of all of the prevalent problems cited for small-group instruction, which do *you* see most commonly? What do you think accounts for this?

4. Are there any other problems and issues with small-group instruction that have not been identified here? What are they?

5. What questions about small-group instruction do you hope to have answered in the next chapter?

Chapter Two

Making Sense of Differentiation

Picture a classroom where instruction is *differentiated*. Do you see children scurrying about, each with an individualized learning plan tucked under their arm, fashioned just for them the evening before by their very dedicated teacher who meticulously matched the next day's learning activities to yesterday's learning outcomes (for all twenty-five of her students)? If this is the image in your mind, you probably concluded long ago that you will never be voted "teacher of the year" because you like to get home from school at least occasionally in time to put your own children to bed at night—and get a couple of hours of sleep yourself. If Disney World ever features a ride through a differentiated classroom, it might look something like this. In real life, however, this classroom rarely exists. And more importantly, this is not even the goal when you're talking about differentiated reading instruction. I propose that we take another look at what actually needs to be differentiated for readers in the intermediate grades—a first step in determining how we will plan and implement our small-group instruction.

THE BUILDING BLOCKS OF DIFFERENTIATION—REVISED

I have long respected Carol Ann Tomlinson as an expert in the area of differentiation. She identifies four instructional components that teachers need to vary in order to meet students' learning needs: content, process, product, and learning environment. (See books by Carol Ann Tomlinson, such as *The Differentiated Classroom: Responding to the Needs of All Learners* and *How to Differentiate Instruction in Mixed-Ability Classrooms*.) For literacy, the rough translation of this is that students read books at different levels of complexity to access core content (content), engage in activities with different degrees of teacher and peer support in accomplishing their learning goals (process), and complete different follow-up tasks as evidence of their achievement (product). All of this would happen within a classroom that accommodated different learning styles (classroom environment).

While these four criteria may be useful for planning differentiated instruction in general (especially within the content areas), I think we need to refine our thinking about them to more specifically target differentiated small-group reading instruction. I will focus on the first three criteria as the classroom environment should *always* accommodate students' individual needs—regardless of the differentiation within the curriculum. This information is presented in three forms: an at-a-glance chart showing the continuum of content, process, and product from high to low literacy performance, a discussion of the most critical dimensions of differentiated reading instruction as identified in the continuum, and a more thorough chart depicting differentiation for readers above grade level, on grade level, and below grade level.

CONTINUUM OF DIFFERENTIATED READING INSTRUCTION IN THE INTERMEDIATE GRADES

HIGH	LOW

CONTENT

Complex text	Simple, clear text
Short and longer text	Mostly short text
Mostly comprehension	Balance comprehension with other literacy needs
Comprehension focus mostly on discussion	Comprehension focus mostly on basic construction of meaning and reinforcing skills and strategies

PROCESS

More independent completion of reading	Reading completed during group time
Brief review of a reading strategy	Reteaching of a strategy that includes explaining and modeling
Little prompting needed to find evidence	More prompting needed
Read longer text chunks/self-monitor	Shorter text chunks to scaffold thinking
Less revisiting of text	More revisiting of text

PRODUCT

Do extensive independent reading of just-right books	Do extensive independent reading of just-right books
Articulate strong personal views about text	Articulate strong personal views about text
Do written response (as needed) independently	Do written response with supports such as answer organizer or answer frame; gradually release responsibility
Do other follow-up tasks independently	Do other follow-up tasks after thorough teacher explaining/modeling with progress monitoring

CONSIDER THE CONTENT

When we think about differentiated reading instruction, the first thing that probably comes to mind is the texts students read. More competent readers get more complex texts; less accomplished readers get texts that are less challenging. Okay, no argument there. But if that's as far as we go with differentiating our content, it is unlikely that we will be doing much to offer readers what they really need. It's not just the books they read—it's what we *do* with the books. It's the way we focus our instruction. We have to get this part right, or all our efforts to plan and implement small-group instruction will have little impact on students' learning.

We recognize that small-group instruction beyond the primary grades needs to focus on comprehension. But saying we're going to "focus on comprehension" is not enough. There are three different ways we can focus our comprehension instruction—and this is the essence of differentiation in the intermediate grades:

- We can focus on constructing basic meaning about a text.

- We can focus on specific comprehension skills and strategies to address particular literacy standards set forth nationally or at a state or district level.

- We can focus on developing students' capacity for discourse to help them think more critically and creatively about text.

When we provide small-group instruction, determining our focus is the most important decision we will make. All students need all three of these focuses—but in different proportions and at different times. High-performing (above-grade-level) students may almost automatically construct basic meaning as they read and thus will need to spend little small-group time reinforcing basic text meaning. We will know this because they will readily summarize what they read. Similarly, these students may not require much in the way of reinforcement of priority literacy objectives—as evidenced by the written responses they produce to open-ended questions assessing literacy standards. Hence, a lot of the small-group time for these students can be used for discussion purposes.

Students performing on or near grade level will also benefit from some time spent on discussion. However, much of their small-group work will probably be focused on reinforcing essential literacy skills and strategies as their open-ended assessment data typically shows "shaky" performance as they strive to meet grade-level literacy standards. Some attention may also be needed on basic construction of meaning leading to skilled summarizing as it is often a lack of fundamental text understanding that gets in the way of achieving mastery on more complex objectives.

Students performing below grade level may spend most of their time just working on basic construction of meaning and producing adequate text summaries before moving on to other (mostly foundational) skills and strategies. In fact, these students may still need to work on word-level skills in their small group. This does not bode well for mastery of high-stakes grade-level expectations and may require additional support in the form of RTI Tier 2 or

Tier 3 interventions beyond what the regular classroom teacher can provide in order to both remediate and accelerate. Nonetheless, these students, too, need the opportunity to hone their discussion skills, and some time should be set aside for this.

CONSIDER THE PROCESS

The "process," with regard to literacy, is mostly about the amount of scaffolding or support that the teacher needs to provide to students. Scaffolding in reading instruction is the means by which teachers gradually release responsibility to students until they can accomplish a task independently. But exactly how will this scaffolding be differentiated? Weaker readers will need to do more reading *during* the small-group session itself so the teacher can directly monitor their performance. While the strategy for reading to find evidence for a particular objective may have been modeled and practiced during a shared lesson with the whole class, the teacher may need to explain and model it again for students who are not so sure how to apply it when they do the reading themselves. Chunks of text that students read will be shorter to catch small misunderstandings before they become big confusions. The teacher also will need to do more prompting to coach students through the process than will be necessary with more capable readers. Concurrently, though, the teacher needs to be especially vigilant with her needy readers to hold them accountable to the standards they *can* achieve and to systematically move them toward greater and greater independence despite their desire for perpetual academic hand-holding. Converting a "can't-do" attitude to "can-do" is one of the biggest challenges faced by teachers differentiating instruction for students who struggle.

While it is certainly true that capable readers will require less of this scaffolding and struggling readers will need more, there are additional ways that the instructional process needs to support students differently. Low-performing students should have the opportunity to read a text or portion of text more than once for different purposes. Actually, *all* students should revisit text more often than they typically do, but this is especially important for strugglers: Maybe they'll read a short story today to construct basic meaning. Tomorrow they might reread it to identify evidence regarding the theme of the story or the lesson a character learned. On a third day, they could pull out powerful passages and work on elements of fluency. Of course, it is not always necessary to read a text three times. But working with a familiar text allows students the chance to dig deeper without constantly having to figure out text basics.

How does the instructional process look different for more advanced readers? In a nutshell, there's more independence. Rather than doing all or most of the reading during the group session itself, more capable readers get a little guidance when the teacher meets with them briefly. Then they go off to read by themselves, applying the focus strategy. Later (that same day or the next day) they return to the group ready to discuss the assigned reading. Occasionally, their instructional focus will be basic construction of meaning. More often, it will be a specific skill or strategy focus or advanced-level discourse.

CONSIDER THE PRODUCT

When referring to literacy, the word *product* doesn't quite work. We see in our mind's eye some kind of culminating project—a poster, a diorama or, in my case, a life-size cardboard cutout of Sara (Plain and Tall). This is the arts-and-crafts view of reading—an activity-based vision of the reading curriculum. What should really count as a *reading product*? At the end of the day, I believe there are two *products* that take precedence over all others: 1) The degree of independence and depth of thinking that students demonstrate as they respond to text both orally and in writing: How well can kids talk and write about what they read? 2) Students' intrinsic motivation to read: Do kids choose to read when given that opportunity among other options?

The deceptive thing about the *product* of students' reading is that we're not seeking to differentiate its *quality*; the plan is for *all* students to be able to talk and write about text in powerful ways. Unless we succeed with this effort, the achievement gap widens instead of narrowing. We will have more—not fewer—children who fail to meet established benchmarks. Similarly, we're hoping that *all* students choose to read when given the chance to do so. The differentiation here is that a "just-right" book for a high-performing student may be more challenging than an independent-level text for a less competent reader. What we hope to differentiate with regard to the end product of reading instruction is the individuality of students' thinking and the breadth of literature they select "just for fun": Will they willingly take a stand on matters of great importance to them suggested in a text? Will they thrive on a wide range of genres or just return to a few old favorites time after time?

For both high- and low-performing students, reading products may also include other related follow-up tasks, including written responses to open-ended comprehension questions. Differentiation here should not be defined by the number of questions students answer—with the high performers getting lots of questions and weaker readers getting fewer. (In fact, everyone should probably get a single question to answer—thoroughly.) What *will* change, though, is the scaffolding and gradual release necessary to get students to independence. In practical terms, that means that less capable readers will need to answer written questions more frequently in order to achieve mastery. They will need more modeling and more extensive use of graphic aids such as answer organizers or answer frames. (See my books, *Teaching Written Response to Text* and *That's a GREAT Answer!* for those scaffolds.) It also means that other follow-up tasks for low readers could incorporate more work with phonics, fluency, and vocabulary in addition to comprehension.

The following chart summarizes differentiation of content, process, and product for above-, on- and below-level readers.

DIFFERENTIATION AT A GLANCE

	Above-level readers	On-level readers	Below-level readers
Content	• Text at or above grade • Many genres • Many authors • Texts of different lengths, including chapter books • Most lessons will focus on comprehension; occasionally other literacy components • More lessons with higher-*level discussion* focus; fewer *constructing basic meaning* or *reinforcing skills and strategies*	• Grade-level text • Introduce (and teach) a variety of genres • Mix of short and longer text • Introduce new authors • Many lessons will focus on comprehension; consistent attention to other literacy components based on data; balance of all 3 areas of focus	• Text may be below grade level • Texts with simple, clear plot structure; clear main ideas • Mostly short text but may include short chapter books • Much attention to comprehension, but the lower the level, the more attention to fluency, word work, and vocabulary • Focus area will most often be *constructing basic meaning or reinforcing skills and strategies* • Below level 20, each small-group lesson should include comprehension, fluency, word work, sight words
Process	• Format will often involve independent completion of task: students come together briefly so teacher can provide short guided practice; students return to seats to read and complete task; students return to group after reading (same day or next day) to discuss reading • Few reminders needed for strategic reading; students should find evidence independently • Read longer chunks of text without "pausing points" established by teacher • Continue reading text independently after group to apply objective from small-group instruction	• Read more challenging texts during group time; other texts may be read more independently (see format for above-level students) • Quickly review strategy for finding evidence for the objective • May need some teacher prompting to find evidence (move toward more independence in this area) • Make sure that "text chunks" are brief enough so students do not lose track of meaning (work toward longer chunks) • Continue reading short amount of text independently after group to apply objective; be sure directions and task are clear	• Read most texts during group time • May need to re-teach objective in step-by-step manner, closely monitoring students' understanding • May need both modeling and prompting to find evidence (be sure to require increasing amounts of independence) • Read text in short chunks and monitor thoroughly after each chunk • Generally will not continue reading text independently after group instruction
Product	• Do extensive amounts of reading independently • Complete written response independently without organizer or frame • Complete follow-up activities independently	• Do substantial amounts of reading independently • Complete written response independently but may require organizer or frame initially; work toward independence • Complete follow-up activities independently after thorough explanation	• Do extensive amounts of independent reading • Complete written response with teacher scaffolding and support from answer organizer or frame; work toward independence • Complete one follow-up activity independently after it has been explained and modeled in the group

If you're one of those teachers who prefers information laid out in very concrete terms ("How will this look in my classroom on Monday morning?"), the chart on the next few pages is for you. I've divided literacy competencies by reading level—approximately— noting how all components of fluent reading will *probably* be integrated into your small-group instruction at various levels. Please recognize that these levels are approximate, with plenty of wiggle room for modifying components at all levels based on teacher judgment.

DIFFERENTIATED SMALL-GROUP INSTRUCTION: INTEGRATING ALL COMPONENTS OF FLUENT READING

On or Below DRA Level 10/Fountas & Pinnell Guided Reading Level F
INSTRUCTIONAL FOCUS
At this level, instruction should be focused on integrating all components of reading (see below) to achieve fluency: phonological awareness, letter recognition, sight words, phonics, fluency, vocabulary, and comprehension. Texts at this level are so limited that the comprehension focus will be almost exclusively *constructing basic meaning*. This will include addressing *story elements* for narrative text *and main idea and details for* informational sources.
COMPONENTS OF FLUENT READING AND HOW TO ADDRESS THEM AT THIS LEVEL
- **Phonological awareness**—Identify students' phonological awareness needs based on an assessment of students' phonological skills. At this level, needs will probably include rhyming (initial consonant substitution) and consonant sounds. Students need to move toward segmenting and blending of sounds.
- **Letter recognition**—Identify letters; distinguish between upper and lower case.
- **Sight words**—Dolch list (flash cards) for kindergarten, pre-primer and primer; sight-word phrases; create phrases/sentences using sight words.
- **Phonics**—Identify students' phonics needs based on the "Developmental Spelling Assessment" found in *Words Their Way* (Templeton, S., et. al., Prentice Hall, 2008) or "Developmental Spelling Inventory" found in *Word Journeys* (Ganske, K., Guilford Publishing, 2000). Use word sorts aligned with assessment data for the *letter name-alphabetic* stage. Students will need extensive focus just on word families (CVC or CVCe).
- **Fluency**—"Whisper read" to teacher to check accuracy and other components of fluency; reread leveled text for accuracy, pace, phrasing; may also use simple poems with repetitive lines.
- **Vocabulary**—Introduce new words one page at a time for immediate transfer. (Most of this vocabulary work will relate to word recognition, not meaning vocabulary.)
- **Comprehension**
  - **Before reading**—Conduct picture walk to establish sense of *story* (narrative) or *topic* (informational). Also make predictions, access prior knowledge, and determine purpose for reading.
  - **During reading**—Read the entire story silently with the teacher "spot-checking" fluency and comprehension by listening in.
  - **After reading**—Review story elements and retell (narrative); review facts learned (informational).

DRA Levels 10-20/Fountas and Pinnell Guided Reading Levels F-K

<u>INSTRUCTIONAL FOCUS</u>

At this level, the instructional intent continues to be the need to integrate all components of fluent reading, so the comprehension focus will be primarily on *constructing basic meaning*. *Reinforcing skills and strategies* and *discourse for higher-level thinking* will be limited by the nature of the texts and the more elementary needs of the students.

- **Constructing basic meaning:** Small-group instruction for students at this level should focus heavily on *constructing basic meaning*, based primarily on *story elements* for narrative text and *main idea and details* for informational sources. A lot of "literature" in this text range is not rich enough to focus meaningfully on comprehension strategies even in a basic way.

- **Reinforcing skills and strategies:** Students reading at this level have a long way to go before meeting grade-level state standards, so any focus on specific skills and strategies will feature very basic objectives: text elements, figuring out the big idea, predicting, determining word meaning from context, identifying beginning/middle/end, finding evidence to support a conclusion. You may sometimes do a focus lesson on vocabulary or fluency, but these needs will generally be addressed in the day-to-day integration of multiple reading components within a small-group lesson (for students reading below level 20.)

- **Discourse for higher-level thinking:** Again, due to the nature of texts at this level, your *higher-level discourse* will be limited. Teachers should ask comprehension questions that correlate with students' reading. But you will probably not plan a lesson at this level solely around higher-level thinking questions.

COMPONENTS OF FLUENT READING AND HOW TO ADDRESS THEM AT THIS LEVEL

- **Phonological awareness**—Identify students' phonological-awareness needs based on an inventory such as the Phonological Awareness Literacy Screening (PALS) or multiple CORE (Consortium of Reading Excellence, Inc.) measures: CORE Phonological Awareness Screening Test, CORE Phoneme Deletion Test, CORE Phonological Segmentation Test, and CORE Phoneme Segmentation Test. At this level, needs will probably include consonant deletion and substitution in initial and final position; rhyming that includes consonant blends/digraphs; and continued work on segmenting and blending.

- **Sight words**—Dolch lists (flash cards) for first grade and second grade; sight-word phrases; create phrases/sentences using sight words; review of pre-primer sight-word list.

- **Phonics**— Identify students' phonics needs based on a *developmental spelling inventory.* Two I like are found in *Words Their Way* (Templeton, S., et. al., Prentice Hall, 2008), and *Word Journeys* (Ganske, K., Guilford Publications, 2000). Use word sorts aligned with assessment data— probably for the *letter name-alphabetic* stage but possibly for introduction of the *within word pattern* stage. Focus areas will likely include short vowel sounds; long vowel sounds; distinguishing between short vowel and long vowel; consonant blends (2 and 3 letters: /sp/, /spl/; consonant digraphs (/th/, /thr/); common vowel digraphs (/ea/, /ai/); common vowel diphthongs (/oo/, /oi/); r-controlled vowels (/ar/, /ir/); easy recognition of CVC and CVCe words.

- **Fluency**—May "whisper read" to teacher, but oral reading to identify evidence is preferable; reread text for accuracy, pace, phrasing, punctuation, expression; poems work well at these levels.

- **Vocabulary**—Introduce new words one page at a time in a leveled text for immediate transfer (most of this vocabulary work will relate to word recognition, not meaning vocabulary).

- **Comprehension**
  - **Before reading**—Look at cover and one or two pictures in the book to make predictions, access prior knowledge, and set purpose for reading; picture walk only if really necessary.
  - **During reading**—Set goal for each page before *silent* reading: identify story elements and make predictions in fiction; identify facts (details) in nonfiction; apply comprehension strategies as appropriate; find evidence to support…

After reading—Review story elements in order to retell/summarize (fiction); identify lesson learned—if appropriate (fiction); review facts learned and determine "big idea" (nonfiction).

DRA Levels 20-30/Fountas & Pinnell Guided Reading Levels K-N

INSTRUCTIONAL FOCUS

At this level, students should have a fairly solid grasp of all of the components that need to be integrated to achieve fluent reading. The instructional focus should turn to comprehension, with other aspects of literacy added in as necessary:

- **Constructing basic meaning:** Almost all small-group instruction for students at this level will need to begin with *constructing basic meaning*. Time can be divided between *story elements* or *sequence of events* (depending on the text structure) and *comprehension strategies (basic)*. It will also be important to incorporate informational text with a focus on *main idea and details*.

- **Reinforcing skills and strategies:** In order for students at this level to meet state standards, much instructional time will need to be spent on reinforcing skills and strategies, especially *specific comprehension objectives*—and it's within the small group that students are likely to make needed progress in this area. Use your data to determine *which* specific *comprehension objectives* and *strategies* need to be reinforced. Be aware, though, that there is often a discrepancy for students at this level between the *symptoms* of comprehension problems and their root *cause*. This means that you will need to determine the prerequisite skills and strategies that may be undermining achievement of grade-level standards—and address these *first* before attempting the comprehension needs that appear on the surface (or those indicated in your grade-level expectations). Regular focus on both *vocabulary* and *fluency* will benefit most students reading within this text range because text complexity is likely to derail comprehension if these areas are weak. Most texts at this level do not contain an abundance of author's crafts, so your focus on this will likely be limited.

- **Discourse for higher-level thinking:** Focus on this as a reread rather than a first read. Again, in order to meet state standards, you will need to spend at least some of your time on *A-D strand questions*; select other questioning techniques aligned with the texts you use. Most leveled texts within this range do not inspire a great deal of critical and creative thinking, so *you* will need to be creative in finding ways for students to engage in higher-level discourse about their reading.

COMPONENTS OF FLUENT READING AND HOW TO ADDRESS THEM AT THIS LEVEL

- **Sight words**—Students may need review of a second-grade sight-word list and instruction on a third-grade list.

- **Word work**—Review students' facility with manipulation of phonetic elements using a strategy such as that described in *Making Words* (Cunningham and Hall) or *Making Big Words* (Cunningham and Hall)) approximately one time per week. This is good for monitoring the way students integrate *all* of their word-level skills. Identify students' word-level needs based on a developmental spelling inventory (such as those noted in Levels 10-20 above). Use word sorts aligned with assessment data—probably for the *within word pattern* stage but possibly for review of the *letter name and alphabetic principle* stage, and introduction of the *syllables and affixes* stage.

- **Fluency**—Read orally to identify evidence; very limited "whisper reading" with the teacher listening in; reread text for accuracy, pace, phrasing, punctuation, expression; choral reading of poems with solo lines or partners; use "fluency phones" for independent practice; may sometimes select fluency as the lesson objective, but fluency will usually be incorporated into *all* lessons in some way.

- **Vocabulary**—Introduce new words a couple of pages at a time for close transfer. Many words will be within students' meaning vocabularies but may need to be highlighted to assure accurate word recognition. There will be some Tier 2 and Tier 3 words as well that you will want to address.

- **Comprehension**
  - **Before reading**—Identify text structure (frequently problem/solution) and review story elements. Be sure that students know they need to find these as they read. If the text is structured as a sequence of events or as main idea and details, make sure students know the difference between these structures and the more typical problem/solution format. Make predictions and access prior knowledge. Establish the purpose (objective) for reading; identify stopping points for reflecting on reading (short passages).
  - **During reading**—Set a goal for each page: "On this page, read to find evidence of…" Students read the text *silently* with oral reading of sentences that verify evidence.

After reading—Review all text elements; review evidence found for meeting the objective; respond to questions *orally* first and then possibly in *writing* (may use answer frame for a while before moving to independence).

DRA Levels 30-40/Fountas and Pinnell Guided Reading Levels N-P

INSTRUCTIONAL FOCUS

At this level, students should be ready for instruction focused on comprehension, with other components of reading incorporated only as necessary:

- **Constructing basic meaning:** For a first read, especially for challenging texts, you will frequently need to focus on *story elements, sequence of events, comprehension strategies (basic)* and *main idea and details*; students at this level may not be ready for a focus on *comprehension strategies (advanced)*.

- **Reinforcing skills and strategies:** In order for students at this level to meet state standards, much instructional time will need to be spent on reinforcing skills and strategies, especially *specific comprehension objectives*—and it's within the small group that students are likely to make needed progress in this area. Use your data to determine *which* specific *comprehension objectives* and *strategies* need to be reinforced; regular focus on both *vocabulary* and *fluency* will benefit students reading within this text range, especially if they are reading below grade level because it's quite possible insufficient vocabulary and/or marginal fluency are negatively impacting their comprehension. Focusing on *author's craft* may not be a priority, but don't overlook a golden opportunity to connect reading and writing when a particular craft really stands out in a text.

- **Discourse for higher-level thinking:** Focus on this as a reread rather than a first read. Again, in order to meet state standards, you will need to spend at least some of your time on *A-D strand questions*; select other questioning techniques aligned with the texts you use. Some leveled texts within this range inspire critical and creative thinking. Make sure you have a worthy text when focusing on discourse.

COMPONENTS OF FLUENT READING AND HOW TO ADDRESS THEM AT THIS LEVEL

- **Word work**—Review students' facility with manipulation of phonetic elements using a strategy such as *making words* or *making big words* approximately once every seven to ten days. This is good for monitoring the way students integrate *all* of their word-level skills. Identify students' word-level needs based on a d*evelopmental spelling inventory*. Use word sorts aligned with assessment data—probably for the *syllables and affixes* stage but possibly for review of the *within word pattern* stage and introduction of the *derivational relations* stage.

- **Fluency**—Read orally to identify evidence—no "whisper reading" or "round-robin reading"; reread text for accuracy, pace, phrasing, punctuation, expression; choral reading of poems with solo lines or partners; reader's theater for reinforcement; may select fluency as a lesson objective for a particular day, though the goal will usually relate to some aspect of comprehension.

- **Vocabulary**—Frontload some vocabulary *before* reading—just two or three words from/about the text that you want students to recognize or think about as they read; explain important words *during* reading that might confuse students; teach lesson on Tier 2 or Tier 3 vocabulary *after* reading.

- **Comprehension**
  - **Before reading**—Identify genre and characteristics of genre; make predictions and access prior knowledge based on author, topic, genre; establish clear purpose (objective) for reading; introduce a few vocabulary words (see above); encourage students to determine their own stopping points to reflect on thinking (finding evidence to meet the objective).

  - **During reading**—Model one or two places where you located evidence for the objective—only as necessary; students read text *silently,* emphasizing finding the evidence independently.

After reading—Review evidence found for meeting the objective; respond to questions *orally* first and then in *writing* if necessary. An answer frame may be necessary at first, but students should be informed from the start that this is not to be a permanent aid—and that there is a clear end point by which independence is expected.

DRA Levels 40-50 (and Above)/Fountas and Pinnell Guided Reading Levels Q-T (and Above)

INSTRUCTIONAL FOCUS

At this level, students should be ready for instruction focused almost exclusively on comprehension with limited time spent on other areas of reading—and only as needed:

- **Constructing basic meaning:** Try to minimize the time spent on *story elements, sequence of events, comprehension strategies (basic)*; continue to focus on *comprehension strategies (advanced)* and *main idea and details*.

- **Reinforcing skills and strategies:** Use your data to determine which specific *comprehension objectives* and *strategies* need to be reinforced to meet state standards; incorporate a focus on *vocabulary* as dictated by the complexity of the text; focus on *fluency* regularly for students who are reading below grade level and occasionally—just for fun—for all students when the text lends itself to dramatic or rhythmic reading; focus on *author's craft* when you spot great places in a text to connect reading and writing through the use of some author's technique.

- **Discourse for higher-level thinking:** Focus on this as often as possible; in order to meet state standards, you will need to spend at least some of your time on *A-D strand questions*; select other questioning techniques aligned with the texts you use (*thinking outside the box* questions for texts that inspire critical thinking; *change it up* questions for creative thinking, etc.). Be sure you are building on students' solid construction of meaning and specific skills and strategies; this may mean that serious discourse is reserved for a reread rather than a first read.

COMPONENTS OF FLUENT READING AND HOW TO ADDRESS THEM AT THIS LEVEL

- **Word work**—Word work at this level will be integrated with vocabulary, especially with regard to the derivational relations of words. Consider using word sorts for this purpose, such as those found in *Words Their Way: Word Sorts for Derivational Relations Spellers* (Templeton, S., et. al., Prentice Hall, 2008).

- **Fluency**—Read orally to identify evidence—no "round-robin" reading; reread text for accuracy, pace, phrasing, punctuation, expression; choral reading of poems with solo lines or partners; reader's theater for reinforcement; read in voices of different characters; may occasionally select fluency as a lesson objective, though the goal will almost always relate to some aspect of comprehension.

- **Vocabulary**—Frontload some vocabulary *before* reading—just two or three words from/about the text that you want students to recognize or think about as they read; explain important words *during* reading that might confuse students; teach lesson on Tier 2 or Tier 3 vocabulary *after* reading.

- **Comprehension**
  - **Before reading**—Identify genre and characteristics of genre; make predictions and access prior knowledge based on author, topic, genre; establish clear purpose (objective) for reading; introduce a few vocabulary words (see above); encourage students to determine their own stopping points to reflect on thinking (finding evidence to meet the objective).

  - **During reading**—Model one or two places where you located evidence for the objective—only as necessary; students read text *silently*, emphasizing finding the evidence independently.

After reading—Review evidence found for meeting the objective; respond to questions *orally* first, and then in *writing* if necessary (if answer frame is needed, it should only be for a day or two).

FROM THINKING TO DOING: DIFFERENTIATED INSTRUCTION IN ACTION

Now that you've rethought the essential features of differentiation in intermediate-grade small-group reading instruction (content, process, and content), consider how these might look in your classroom. Use the template on page 27, *Differentiated Instruction in the Intermediate Grades*, to decide how small-group instruction might be different for different groups of your students.

Another way to try your hand at differentiation is to look at some hypothetical groups of students: How would you address their needs—not just in a single lesson, but over three days? Look at the descriptions on page 28, *What Will I Teach and How Will I Teach It?* Choose a text familiar to you and plot your teaching over three sessions using the *Three-Day Small-Group Reading Plan* on page 30. For now, just think about the needs of these students in terms of content, process, and product. After you learn about all of the instructional formats that follow in Part II of this book, come back to this exercise and decide which focus might work best with a particular group. There are sixteen different focuses, so you will have many from which to choose. (Use this template as you plan instruction for your own students, too.)

	High	Middle	Low
Content			
Process			
Product			

WHAT WILL I TEACH AND HOW WILL I TEACH IT? SCENARIOS FOR PLANNING SMALL-GROUP INSTRUCTION OVER THREE DAYS

1. This group of six fourth graders is reading approximately on grade level. Two of the students (both girls) are not native English speakers. However, they no longer receive services from the ESOL teacher. Their academic vocabulary still lags behind that of their peers in subtle ways, which sometimes gets in the way of their comprehension. Another two students in this group are boys who do not enjoy reading. Fluency is not a problem, but they barely scratch the surface in terms of text meaning. They rarely participate in group discussion—and then only when the teacher asks them a direct question. The fifth student, also a boy, likes to read but dislikes writing about his reading. The last child, a girl, received reading support in the past but is now on track. The issue with her is that she wants to do *all* the talking during the group.

2. This group of four third graders includes students at various reading levels—all substantially below grade expectancy. One student is reading on a level 14. Two are on level 16, and the fourth is a level 18. They all currently receive Tier 2 intervention, though their (scripted) program focuses mostly on comprehension rather than issues undermining their reading fluency. Their word-level skills are seriously deficient. They handle CVC and CVEe words pretty well. But vowel combinations and words with more than one syllable cause problems every time! The level 18 student makes an effort to use visual cues, but the remaining children continue to rely heavily on picture clues and outright guessing—even when those strategies do not help them make sense of the text. The lowest student has difficulty retaining sight words and recognizing them in connected reading. To make matters worse, the state test is only two months away and these students struggle with priority comprehension objectives such as summarizing a story and making personal connections.

3. This group of five above-level fifth graders is a pleasure to work with—if only you had enough time to work with them. With so many needy students in your classroom, you frequently hand these students a packet of questions about more difficult chapter books. You do meet with them about once a week to check their answers, but there's never enough time to engage in the kind of conversation that could really extend these students' thinking. And you worry that you're not even asking the right questions. You recently had the good fortune of acquiring the services of a paraprofessional for two thirty-minute periods during the week. You've decided that you will make use of this extra help by asking this para to do some follow-up work with a couple of your lower groups so you can devote more effort to these high readers. But what will your "kicked-up" instruction look like?

4. It is April of second grade, and you have a group of six students reading at approximately a DRA level 30. They decode easily and their fluency is quite good. Now if they could only comprehend what they read! They have an especially hard time with nonfiction although, honestly, they struggle with basic story retelling, too. These are capable children who should be able to reach goal on grade-level standards. But at this rate, you are worried about them and wonder if at least one (an English learner) will slip behind grade-level peers and into a lower group. One more thing: these children dutifully do their work and enjoy their reputation as "the highest group." But only one little boy in this group is what you'd call a "reader"; you can tell he reads at night and over the weekend. The others: not so much.

5. This year, your urban school is trying something new: single-sex classrooms. You are teaching a whole class of fourth-grade boys and, in the spirit of this experiment, you boldly decided to throw caution to the wind and meet with students in small groups based on *interests* rather than *reading level*. You've pulled together a group of six students (DRA levels 30-44) who say they like animals—though not necessarily *reading* about animals. All of these exuberant boys need work on comprehension. (They miss key details and then the larger meaning.) Two of the boys need better fluency. (Too much word-by-word reading.) And vocabulary? (The real issue here is lack of background knowledge on many topics.) How can you harness this "boy power" to build better reading skills and greater reading engagement in your classroom?

6. This group of five sixth-grade students is comprised of three boys and two girls reading slightly below grade level. They struggle with higher-level thinking, almost anything beyond literal-level questions with answers that can be found right on the page. These students also tend to produce written responses to open-ended questions that are more sparse than specific, which further reduces their perception as competent readers—as well as the likelihood that they will do well on the upcoming state assessment. One strength of these students is that they like to talk (as long as the conversation achieves their social purposes in addition to the intended academic focus). So…what to do with these students? They need skills. They need strategies. They need to *care* about their reading. Yep, these are just typical middle-school kids putting in the requisite seat time in their language arts class.

7. These four third graders love to read. They are reading just about on grade level—level 34—midway through the year. Sometimes their enthusiasm outdistances their fluency; *fast* reading seems to be their goal, with too little attention to punctuation, phrasing, and expression. A focus on speed sometimes gets in the way of their comprehension, too. They miss supporting evidence in a text and then can't figure out the "big idea." These kids need a regular diet of all of the literacy components that contribute to reading competence. How can you structure a sequence of lessons that will lead ultimately to this goal?

THREE-DAY SMALL-GROUP READING PLAN

GRADE LEVEL: _____   READING LEVEL: _____

DAY 1

Focus	Content (text)	Process (What will students do during the lesson?)	Product (What will students be able to do following the lesson?)

DAY 2

Focus	Content (text)	Process (What will students do during the lesson?)	Product (What will students be able to do following the lesson?)

DAY 3

Focus	Content (text)	Process (What will students do during the lesson?)	Product (What will students be able to do following the lesson?)

MOVING FORWARD

In order to be proactive rather than reactive to intermediate-grade students' small-group reading needs, we need to begin with an understanding of small-group basics, finding answers to those questions that immediately come to mind when we hear the term "small-group instruction." Answers to these frequently asked questions follow in Chapter Three. Before moving forward, though, consider how you might answer the questions below about problems you confront when considering your small-group instructional needs.

QUESTIONS TO CONSIDER

1. Before reading this chapter, what was your perception of differentiation, especially as it related to small-group instruction?

2. Do you feel less stressed about differentiation now? Why or why not?

3. Was there a particular "ah-ha" moment in this chapter that will help you rethink small-group instruction?

4. A big issue in differentiation is the need to consider the needs of readers beyond just their reading level. In what ways did this chapter help you address this need?

5. What do you look forward to learning in Part II of this book?

Chapter Three

Frequently Asked Questions About Small-group Instruction

Before moving forward with all those instructional formats for small groups, let's step back for a moment and answer some very basic questions, all common concerns of teachers about to embark on small-group instruction. These responses should answer your general questions. More specific questions related to *your* students, *your* data, and *your* schedule will need to be addressed by someone in *your* building. To whom will you go with your more pointed questions? Tapping the right resource makes all the difference in getting the information you need to effectively implement a new teaching practice. As you read the questions and answers below, think about whose help you might seek to launch your small groups with competence and confidence.

HOW DO I PLACE MY STUDENTS INTO GROUPS?

There are a couple of principles that I believe ought to guide your thinking as you create groups. First, students need to be able to read text at an *instructional* level. This means that the text will be more challenging than a "just-right" book that they would read independently—but not so challenging that they can't read it fluently; in other words, lack of word-level skills should *not* get in the way of comprehension.

Your assessment data will help you determine where to place students. Remember, though, that nothing is more reliable than your day-to-day observations of children as you work with them in shared, guided, and independent reading. In my view, the best use of data is to confirm what you think you already know. And when it offers up a surprise, dig a little deeper with appropriate assessments to either confirm or adjust your initial thinking.

Can you "stretch" students to place them in one group or another? Absolutely. Remember that beyond the primary grades, text gradient becomes much harder to nail down. Whether a student can—and will—read a particular text is based a lot on prior knowledge of the topic, personal interest, and other factors that we are disinclined to acknowledge and that nonetheless do make a difference: Is there a cool picture on the front cover? Are the chapters too long or too short? Do they like the author? Did their best friend read the book? So, you can often place students together who do read at somewhat different levels—say a DRA 34 with a 40—if the topic is one that entices and you are willing to support different readers differently.

Recognize, however, that there will be a point where motivation alone will not compensate for lack of skills. In a recent workshop when we were discussing grouping options, one teacher offered, "You could even put a level 12 with a level 40 as long as the topic is suitable." Well, no, you really can't. That's just too great a spread. A student with a DRA of 12 won't be able to handle the complexities of a level 40 text.

HOW OFTEN SHOULD MY GROUPS CHANGE?

Unlike days of yore when "once a Bluebird, always a Bluebird," your groups will be a bit more fluid. As you reassess, you can (and should) regroup. If your groups are the same in June as they were in September, you probably haven't made very good use of your data or day-to-day knowledge of your readers. On the other hand, I'm not promoting what has come to be known as "flexible grouping" here either. In flexible grouping, the teacher pulls a group of students today who may need more work on making text-to-self connections. Tomorrow maybe some of these same students and a few additional kids come together to work on inferring character traits. This kind of grouping is temporary, reflective of an in-the-moment need. This sounds reasonable enough—except that the small-group work conducted in this way is sporadic at best. Some students may have the opportunity to work together with a group of their peers only rarely. And worst-case scenario, this is too much trouble to manage—and small groups don't happen at all. (Flexible grouping was, to the best of my memory, an invention a couple of decades ago of mega, one-size-fits-all core programs that needed to offer up some attempt at differentiation, meager though this was.)

I think it's important to remember that a critical component of small-group instruction is the group experience itself. Think about your own participation in a book club. Half the fun of that is getting to know the thinking of other group members on a more personal level. If different people showed up each time, would you bond enough to share close-to-your-heart thoughts and feelings about a book? It's the same for kids; you need a certain comfort level with other readers in order to trust them with your thinking.

So, groups should change when they need to change. Most frequently, this will be dictated by student performance. But interest could also play a role. Perhaps the next reading focus will be a study of biography. If you have a few texts that many students could read, give them some choice: Who wants to read about Marian Anderson? Rosa Parks? Jackie Robinson? The trick is to make sure that all student choices will ultimately be *good* choices; your careful planning and text selection will ensure that.

HOW MANY GROUPS SHOULD I HAVE—AND HOW MANY STUDENTS ARE APPROPRIATE FOR EACH GROUP?

In theory, four groups in the intermediate grades works well. This, however, is based on some assumptions about your class that may or may not be accurate. It assumes that you have no more than about twenty-four students in your class. It assumes that students will divide themselves neatly into groups of approximately the same size (six or so students in each group). It assumes that you do not have "outliers"—a student here or there who is significantly above or below the level of other groups, requiring you to meet with this child individually.

Rather than work with too many groups (I really think five or more groups at the intermediate level is too many), the better course of action is to combine students who are close enough in level, with the realization that you will need to support different students differently within the same group. "Great," you're probably wondering. "How close is close enough?" Assessment data aside, the main question you need to answer is: Is this text at students' *instructional* level? Consider: Will word-level issues get in the way of comprehension? Is the complexity of the text about right for students to grasp conceptually? If you can answer both of these questions affirmatively, go ahead and place children together.

Teachers sometimes argue with me that they couldn't *possibly* get all their kids into just four groups. But closer analysis, perhaps another pair of eyes to rethink the situation—maybe those of a literacy coach or an administrator—often tells a different story. Beware of a possible hidden agenda here. Having too many groups becomes an "easy out" when you need to justify why you're not meeting with some groups as regularly as you should be.

HOW OFTEN—AND FOR HOW LONG—SHOULD I MEET WITH EACH GROUP?

This is basically a math problem. How many minutes do you have available for small-group instruction? If you have sixty or more minutes, as I hope you do, you can meet three groups for twenty minutes apiece. Or you can see all four groups—two of them for the full twenty minutes and the remaining two for a shorter period, just to get them started. Students in the "short groups" today will sit with you just long enough to get started on a task they will complete at their seats; tomorrow they will participate in a full-length group to reflect on today's reading. This approach works well if you have students in your class capable of independence. If *all* of your children need your careful guidance as they read, you may get to only three groups in an hour period. While you may prefer to meet with students for thirty minutes (after all, you're having this fabulous discussion…), resist this urge and discipline yourself to send them back to their seats when their allotted twenty-minute session is up. Meeting with only two groups per day will mean that you see each group too few times during the week. And meeting with only one group per day renders your small-group work almost useless. You need to meet with groups of struggling readers *every* day. Try to meet with average groups at least four times each week. Advanced readers should have the opportunity to participate in a full group a minimum of three days weekly.

WHEN AND WHERE WILL SMALL-GROUP INSTRUCTION TAKE PLACE?

Ideally your small-group instruction will happen right after shared reading. This is perfect because students are then more likely to recognize the connection between the objective they addressed in the shared lesson and the carryover (for many students) of the same objective into their small-group work. I also push for all reading instruction to occur in the morning when students' thinking is the freshest. If morning isn't an option, aim for early afternoon. Of course, it's great to have one nice, long literacy block. But this isn't always possible. Breaking your reading time into two parts actually works pretty well sometimes because too long a stretch doing any one thing is tough on kids with short attention spans.

One of the first things I look for when visiting a classroom is a space conducive to small-group work. My first choice is a round table. Remember how King Arthur proposed this for Camelot? All the knights would be equal. That's a good idea for children, too; no one (not even the teacher) gets the "seat of honor." A rectangular table would be my next choice. Last choice would be one of those kidney-shaped tables that we all fought so hard to acquire not that long ago. That little indentation in the middle spells out very clearly who's in charge. Additionally, it's impossible to focus visually on your entire group at once. And the kids to your left can barely see the kids to your right—a real disadvantage when you're trying to have a discussion.

There are a few folks out there who don't think you should have *any* table for small-group instruction; just settle yourselves on the rug or in a huddle of chairs. If this works for you—no problem. Personally, I think they're carrying this egalitarian thing a tad too far! Getting up from the floor is a challenge for some teachers. And without a table, students have to balance their books on their laps along with anything else they might have brought with them to their group.

WHEN SHOULD I BEGIN MY SMALL-GROUP INSTRUCTION?

The short answer to this is: as soon as possible! Another reason teachers give for no small-group instruction is that they have not yet finished assessing their students. In November? If we're spending two months testing when we should be teaching, it's no wonder students don't make a year's worth of academic progress in a year. After two weeks in the third grade or whatever grade—with or without formal assessment—teachers who have consistently worked with their students on literacy ought to have a reasonably accurate estimate of their reading needs. Place them in tentative groups. What's the worst that can happen? You might need to move a few kids around. This is certainly preferable to biding your time until you've sifted through mountains of data.

WHAT WILL THEY READ?

The instructional formats that follow identify text types that work well for different purposes. The common thread that dominates throughout is that teachers need to use more short text in their small groups. This can be poems, short stories, informational articles, excerpts from longer texts—anything that can be read in a session or two. This allows many passes through the same process to reinforce a skill or strategy. That said, you can't completely ignore longer texts—chapter books or other materials that may take a week or more to read. Longer books offer more complex text structures, multiple themes, richer characters. Beware, however, of the chapter book that is likely to take students several weeks to read. Instead, use those books for read-alouds, where the experience will move along more quickly because the intent is simply enjoyment.

"But I don't have enough leveled books," you worry. This need not be a deterrent. You can easily tell whether a book is too hard for a student by asking him to read aloud a passage of approximately one hundred words. Technically, accuracy should be at least ninety-five percent at the instructional level, with about eighty percent comprehension on simple recall questions. That means that students will not stumble over more than five words in that passage. Personally, I believe the accuracy rate should be higher, more like ninety-eight percent, for the instructional level. If a student misreads more than two words in a short text segment of just one hundred words, imagine the number of words she will probably miss on an entire page—and the impact this is likely to have on comprehension.

WHAT WILL THE REST OF THE CLASS DO WHILE I'M WORKING WITH MY SMALL GROUP?

I wish I had a quarter for every time a teacher has asked me this question. One absolute non-negotiable is that every intermediate-grade child should engage in at least twenty minutes of independent reading every day. More is fine; less is not. This is not SSR (sustained silent reading), where students read whatever they feel like reading with absolutely no accountability. This is a significant component of the literacy curriculum where all students read a "just-right" book at their independent level to apply reading strategies and skills *on their own*. They may simply record the pages read in a reading log. Or they may respond in a reader's notebook in the manner they choose. They should also be prepared to talk about their independent reading when the whole class convenes at the end of the morning to reflect on the day's literacy learning.

During this workshop period, students can get needed practice in other areas of literacy, too: fluency, vocabulary, written response, word work. Should this happen in literacy "centers?" I'm not for or against centers. I'm for authentic reading and writing. If there's a reason for students to come together in a special place to accomplish that work—for example, to engage in reader's theater—that makes a lot of sense. If, however, several students are sitting around the same table filling out identical vocabulary skill sheets, this seems a poor excuse for a "center."

The reason this workshop period is scary to teachers is that they anticipate the need for massive amounts of differentiation. If you plot out the minutes, you will see that the time is too short to get crazed over this. Here's how I see the hour breaking down:

LITERACY WORKSHOP PERIOD: 60 MINUTES

20 minutes: Small-group instruction

20 minutes: Independent reading

20 minutes: Follow-up activity from shared reading, follow-up activity from small-group instruction, reader's notebook response, other writing, vocabulary, fluency, word work

---

As you can see, the time is almost too short; you and you and your students will have little difficulty filling it with meaningful reading and writing. If this happens to be a day when you are not working with a particular group, add a few additional minutes of independent reading or reading related to the small-group text. This workshop period should not be an occasion to haul out large quantities of activities that come in a box.

MOVING FORWARD

You probably have some additional questions about small-group instruction that I have not answered. My best advice is to just get started. As with so many things in education, you have much more knowledge and know-how than you think you do. As you apply some of the principles explained here and implement a few of the formats in the following chapters, you will, in fact, answer your questions yourself.

Armed with a broader view of typical problems that teachers face in implementing small-group instruction in the intermediate grades (Chapter One), the essence of differentiation of instructional practices (Chapter Two), and answers to frequently asked questions about the nuts and bolts of small-group instruction (Chapter Three), you are now ready to embark on your exploration of the sixteen instructional formats that will make all of this work. Before you begin this journey, however, reflect on the questions below.

QUESTIONS TO CONSIDER

1. What questions remain for you? Are these issues you could figure out for yourself, or do you need assistance? Who could you ask?

2. Who is the go-to person in your building who could best answer your specific questions about small-group instruction—administrator? Coach? Literacy consultant? Another classroom teacher?

3. Do you have anything to add to the responses in this chapter? Explain.

4. What do you think is the most important question about small-group instruction?

Part II:

Implementing Small-group Instruction: A Menu of Possibilities

Introduction
to Part II

The remainder of this book provides sixteen wonderful ways to implement small-group instruction in your classroom—in four very comprehensive chapters. While you may be tempted to try them all in short order, that would probably be a mistake. Instead, read through them to get an overview, then focus on a couple of formats at a time that show promise for your students. Implement them until you and your students feel comfortable with the process. Feel free to adapt them, too. These are *your* small groups, and you will find variations that will make these strategies work optimally in your classroom.

To get a sense of the big picture, look at the chart on page 42, *Small-group Instruction at a Glance*. The chapters ahead are organized according to these chart categories and provide you with the information you need to answer the following questions for each focus:

- What's the purpose?
- Who would benefit from this focus?
- What kinds of texts should I use?
- What resources will I need for teaching and assessing?
- How do I implement this?
- How do I measure students' success?

The ultimate goal by the end of this book is to understand how formats differ from each other based on the specifics of each instructional focus. It is this understanding that will help you differentiate your instruction for maximum impact on student learning.

To help you plan for your small-group instruction, see the *Small-group Planner* on page 43. I spent a lot of time devising this, trying to strike a balance between *no* planning—which I'm sad to say characterizes small-group instruction in some classrooms that I've visited—and the need for *too much writing*, which is a real turn-off for busy teachers. I settled on a form comprised mostly of little boxes to check—with just a bit of writing (to make sure you've thought through the implementation of your plan in a concrete way).

Finally, on pages 44-48, I've included an annotated *Bibliography of Short Texts* as additional support since I advocate the use of short text so strongly in many of the chapters ahead. This bibliography does not include leveled texts offered by textbook publishing companies. Rather, these are authentic texts by authors you and your students will recognize.

SMALL-GROUP INSTRUCTION AT A GLANCE

Focus	Purpose	Who Benefits	Texts	Resources	Implementation	Assessment
Constructing Basic Meaning						
Story Elements						
Sequence of Events						
Main Idea and Details						
Comprehension Strategies (Basic)						
Comprehension Strategies (Advanced)						
Reinforcing Skills and Strategies						
Specific Comprehension Objectives						
Specific Comprehension Strategies						
Fluency						
Vocabulary						
Author's Craft						
Discourse for Higher-level Thinking						
A-D Strand Questions						
Comprehension Strategy Questions						
Thinking Outside the Box						
Creative-thinking Questions						
Informational Text Questions						

SMALL-GROUP PLANNER: _____

Group

DATE: _____ **TEXT:** _____ **PAGES:** _____

Constructing Basic Meaning
❏ Story Elements   ❏ Sequence of Events   ❏ Main Idea and Details
❏ Comprehension Strategies (Basic)   ❏ Comprehension Strategies (Advanced)

Reinforcing Skills and Strategies
❏ Specific Comprehension Objective: _____
❏ Specific Comprehension Strategy: _____
❏ Specific Author's Craft: _____
      ❏ Fluency   ❏ Vocabulary

Discourse for Higher-level Thinking
❏ A-D Strand Questions   ❏ Comprehension Strategy Questions
❏ Informational Text Questions   ❏ Thinking Outside the Box (Critical Thinking)
❏ Change It Up (Creative Thinking)

◎ **Students will be able to** _____ **by** _____
_____

During the lesson, students will:
   1.

   2.

   3.

Follow-up task: _____

Notes about students:

ANNOTATED BIBLIOGRAPHY OF SHORT TEXTS SUITABLE FOR ADDRESSING COMPREHENSION

Finding short text for small-group instruction is not always the easiest task, especially if you're looking for short stories appropriate for elementary students. I've been collecting the following books for a decade or longer. Finding texts for middle school is easier, with anthologies focused on everything from frogs to fables to multicultural neighborhoods—and everything in between. Many of these anthologies beg the question: how short is a short story? *Short* can be as brief as a single page or as long as twenty to thirty pages. Some of these stories can be read in one sitting; others may need up to a week. For the most part, even a "longish" short story will be shorter than a "shortish" novel. I've divided texts into two levels because of the subject matter they typically address: **intermediate (approximately grades three-six)** and **middle school (approximately grades five-eight)**. Use the grade levels noted below as guidelines, adjusting them up or down for the students you teach.

I

Intermediate (approximately grades three-six)

There are at least some small anthologies with short texts students can read for themselves at this level. Within any one of these books, some stories might work for the students in your grade while others might be better suited to students older or younger. Text complexity in an anthology seems to vary quite a bit.

M

Middle School (approximately grades five-eight)

There are many anthologies of short stories and poetry available to students at the middle-school level, and they are generally very high quality. In lots of cases, a single anthology is a compilation of stories authored by multiple well-known authors of adolescent literature all addressing a common theme. The stories and poems capture in just a few pages the essence of issues confronted by young teens from many different cultures worldwide.

Short Stories	I	M
America Street: A Multicultural Anthology of Stories edited by Anne Mazer: These 14 stories describe the experience of growing up in our diverse society—as a Native American, Asian, Latino, European, African, Arab, and Jew. All are finding their way, facing the realities of home, school, and friendship. Stories are 10+ pages.		x
American Dragons: Twenty-five Asian-American Voices edited by Laurence Yep: The stories in this book celebrate the Asian-American experience, although their messages in each speak to *all* adolescents. Stories are about 10 pages.		x
Baseball in April and Other Stories by Gary Soto: In this collection of stories, the small events of daily life reveal big themes—love and friendship, youth and growing up, etc. The kids in these stories are Latino, but their dreams belong to all adolescents. Stories are about 10 pages.		x
Birthday Surprises edited by Johanna Hurwitz: This is prompt writing at its best! The editor sent various children's authors this prompt: *You receive a beautifully wrapped book for your birthday—and discover it is empty. Write the story that follows.* The results are diverse, indeed. Ten stories between 8-12 pages.	x	x
Chicken Soup for the Kid's Soul: 101 Stories of Courage, Hope, and Laughter edited by Jack Canfield, et. al.: These brief vignettes about growing up are by kids, for kids. Most vignettes are 2-3 pages.	x	x
Chicken Soup for the Teenage Soul: 101 Stories of Life, Love, and Learning edited by Jack Canfield, Mark Hansen, and Kimberly Kirberger: This volume includes many short vignettes about surviving and succeeding during the teen years while maintaining both your sanity and your sense of humor. Vignettes are typically 2-4 pages.		x
Dog to the Rescue: Seventeen True Tales of Dog Heroism by Jeanette Sanderson: These are true stories of courage and friendship between humans and their dogs. Each story is about 5 pages.	x	x
Every Living Thing by Cynthia Rylant: Every story in this lovely little anthology focuses on an animal—in a very positive way. Classic Rylant. One of my favorite books of short text. 12 stories of approximately 6-8 pages each.	x	x
Fables by Arnold Lobel: These updated fables are humorous with a lesson to be learned in each one. Different fables will be appreciated by different grade levels. VERY short—a single page each.	x	x
Five True Dog Stories by Margaret Davidson: These stories about real dogs have great kid appeal (includes *Balto, the Dog Who Saved Nome*). The reading level of these stories is 2.0, although they don't look like "baby books"—great for older struggling readers. (There are also *Five True Dolphin Stories; Cat Stories; Horse Stories*.) Stories are about 8-10 pages.	x	

Short Stories	I	M
Guys Write for Guys Read compiled by Jon Scieszka: The vignettes in this book—92 of them—describe guy moments—funny, humiliating, sad, triumphant. There's something here for every kind of *guy*, and girls will enjoy these, too. Each vignette is 2-3 pages.		x
Hey World, Here I Am! by Jean Little: In about 50 very short vignettes and poems, Kate Bloomfield, an outspoken middle-school-age kid, uses her very outspoken voice to share her honest feelings about school, friends, parents, and life's random moments. Entries are about 1-2 pages.		x
Indian Shoes by Cynthia Leitich Smith: 6 interrelated stories written with humor about what it is like to grow up as a Seminole-Cherokee boy. Stories are about 10 pages with fairly large font.	x	
It's Fine to Be Nine (Scholastic): This book contains excerpts from popular children's books, such as *Ramona Forever, Pippi Longstocking, The Chalkbox Kid*, etc. Each chapter is 10-15 pages.	x	
Listen Children: An Anthology of Black Literature edited by Dorothy Strickland: This introduction to the world of black literature contains 22 pieces—stories, poems, a play, even the most famous speech of Martin Luther King, Jr. Varying lengths.	x	x
Local News compiled by Gary Soto: In this collection of 13 stories, the author captures the nuances of growing up in a Mexican-American neighborhood. Stories are about 10 pages.		x
New Kids in Town: Oral Histories of Immigrant Teens by Janet Bode: There are 12 stories in this anthology, each told in the voice of an immigrant teen from a different country. Stories are about 10 pages.		x
Past Perfect, Present Tense by Richard Peck: Not only are the stories in this text exceptional, but the author includes a great introduction to the book about what a short story is and is not. Stories are about 10 pages.		x
Point of Departure: 19 Stories of Youth and Discovery edited by Robert Gold: The stories in this collection probe the mystery, love, pain, and affirmation of adolescent lives. Stories are about 10 pages.		x
Read-Aloud Anthology edited by Janet Allen: This anthology with 35 very short stories, nonfiction articles, poems, and speeches is a great mix of many different kinds of texts. Each piece is about 2-5 pages.		x
Ribbiting Tales edited by Nancy Springer: In this book, 8 favorite children's authors have each written a story that features a frog. Some are fanciful; some are realistic. All are fun! Stories are 10+ pages.	x	
Shelf Life: Stories by the Book edited by Gary Paulsen: Gary Paulsen invited 10 children's authors to write a short story to be included in this anthology. But there was a catch: each story had to mention a book in some way. Stories are 10+ pages.		x

Short Stories	I	M
Some of the Kinder Planets by Tim Wynne-Jones: These wise and witty stories feature 9 ordinary kids cast in offbeat situations who manage to create something magical from them—while in search of their own place in the universe. Stories are 10 + pages.		x
Stay True: Short Stories for Strong Girls compiled by Marilyn Singer: 11 distinguished authors explore issues like generational differences, independence, abuse, and relationships. These stories are both inspiring and entertaining. Stories are about 20 pages.		x
The Kingfisher Treasury of Stories for Seven Year Olds chosen by Edward and Nancy Blishen: These 19 stories from around the world (mostly fairytales) will appeal to young children—though young children won't necessarily be able to read them by themselves. Most stories are 4-5 pages.	x	
The Fabled Fourth Graders of Aesop Elementary School by Candace Fleming: These modern-day fables set in a fourth-grade classroom come complete with a moral—and plenty of humor, too. 15 fables, each about 5 pages.	x	
The Stone Soup Book of Friendship Stories (student writers; published by Scholastic): These stories are written by students in their early teens around the theme of friendship. Stories are about 5 pages.	x	x
They Led the Way: 14 American Women by Johanna Johnston: The women described in this book are proof that the world has many places and possibilities for women as well as for men. Stories are about 10 pages.	x	
Thirteen edited by James Howe: 12 stories and one poem by contemporary writers of teen fiction capture the agony and ecstasy of being 13. Most stories are 20-25 pages.		x
Twelve Impossible Things Before Breakfast by Jane Yolen: These modern myths and tales transform the impossible into *almost* familiar and real. Some of the tales are scary; others cross or fanciful. All are great feasts for the imagination. 12 stories; 10+ pages.		x
Two-Minute Mysteries by Donald Sobol: These very brief vignettes are great for helping students notice key pieces of evidence—essential in solving each mystery. Each mystery is 2 pages.	x	x
What Do Fish Have to Do with Anything? by Avi: These 7 stories chart the turning points in the lives of each protagonist. There's always an angle or some surprise the reader does not expect. EXCELLENT stories and great for a theme study about personal turning points! Stories are about 20-30 pages.		x

Poetry	I	M
By Definition: Poems of Feelings by Sara Holbrook (and several other short poetry books: *Living on the Boundaries of Change; It's Not the End of the World; The Dog Ate My Homework; Am I Naturally this Crazy?*): Holbrook conveys the angst of being a young teen, sometimes with humor, always with a dose of reality.		x
Dear Mother, Dear Daughter by Jane Yolen and Heidi Stemple: This mother-daughter duo writes letters back and forth to each other on such issues as cleaning one's bedroom, practicing your musical instrument, and going to the mall. Messages from both parties ring true.		x
Dirty Laundry Pile: Poems in Different Voices selected by Paul Janeczko: Short poems written in the voices of objects such as a scarecrow, snowflake, kite, etc.	x	x
Dizzy in Your Eyes: Poems about Love by Pat Mora: These 50 poems describe love for a boyfriend, a girlfriend, a family, a pet, a sport, and music. Has anyone ever felt like this before? All love feels like a first love.		x
Hormone Jungle: Coming of Age in Middle School by Brod Bagert: More middle-school humor and angst in this poetry anthology that looks more like a kid's scrapbook. Great graphic appeal.		x
Meet Danitra Brown by Nikki Grimes: This series of poems about friendship set in an urban environment is written in the voice of Danitra's best friend Zuri and depicts the strong friendship that these girls share.	x	
My Man Blue by Nikki Grimes: These poignant poems communicate the challenges of urban life through the friendship of a child and an older man.	x	x
My Name Is Jorge on Both Sides of the River by Jane Medina: The powerful poems in this book are written in both English and Spanish. They resonate with the complex emotions of the English language learners in our classrooms.	x	x
Poetry for Young People: Langston Hughes edited by David Roessel and Arnold Rampersad: This anthology is part of a series of books about various poets. Each poem is preceded by a brief description that sets its context. And the accompanying illustrations are fabulous! Different poems would be appropriate for different grade levels.	x	x
Poetry for Young People: Maya Angelou edited by Edwin Graves Wilson: This is another book in the series above. I recommend *all* of these anthologies, which also include poets Robert Frost, Walt Whitman, and Emily Dickinson.	x	x
The Flag of Childhood: Poems from the Middle East selected by Naomi Shihab Nye: Poems from Palestine, Israel, Egypt, Iraq, and elsewhere open windows into the hearts and souls of people we generally encounter only on the nightly news. These poems explore the human connections beneath the veil of stereotypes.		x

Chapter Four

Constructing Basic Meaning:
The Prequel

THE PREQUEL: PART I—COMPREHENSION STRATEGIES

I was amused when I received an email recently from a principal in another state about the workshop she wanted me to provide for her K-3 staff. The title on the attached flyer in big, bold print announced: "Constructing Meaning: The Prequel." The back story on this is that I had done another presentation for this district earlier in the year about my book, *Launching RTI Comprehension Instruction with Shared Reading* (Maupin House, 2009). It was news to teachers in this district as I talked with them that day that there were other books I had written before this one. And so, after the workshop, they had apparently gotten busy checking out my other books and had obtained multiple copies of *Constructing Meaning through Kid-Friendly Comprehension Strategy Instruction* (Maupin House, 2004). The principal saw this as foundational knowledge that ought to precede the development of more focused comprehension objectives, such as those identified in the *Launching* book. It was very smart of this principal to recognize this! Now she wanted me to come back to help her teachers become more skilled in delivering instruction around the comprehension strategies that led to basic construction of meaning.

We should never underestimate the importance of constructing basic meaning about a text. In their zeal to address high-stakes state literacy standards, teachers sometimes assume students "get" the general meaning, and are too quick to move on to more advanced objectives requiring higher-level thinking—determining the theme, delving deeper into character analysis, identifying the most important part. But can they summarize what they just read? If not, you might as well forget about achieving those loftier goals.

Here's the tricky part: While it is true that the capacity to summarize is a reliable indicator of students' basic construction of meaning about a text, the answer to this dilemma does not lie simply in teaching kids to create better summaries. That would be too easy! As with so many issues in education, the real deal is not what you see on the surface, but what lurks beneath. When you focus only on "how do you write a good summary?" you are addressing the *symptom*. What you need to focus on instead is the *cause*: What is getting in the way of students' ability to summarize?

The "prequel principal" was on the right track: Let's teach them to monitor their thinking using comprehension strategies so that when they finish reading a text, they *can* construct basic meaning. Two of the small-group instructional frameworks that follow in this chapter explain ways to focus on comprehension strategies: one at a very basic level, ***Comprehension Strategies—Basic***, which can be used with students of *all* levels, and a second approach to using strategies, ***Comprehension Strategies—Advanced***, which is geared to more advanced readers engaged in more sophisticated text.

Both of these approaches incorporate the "kid-friendly" strategy labels I introduced in my *Constructing Meaning* book so that the language of strategy use is accessible to *all* learners. This is a perfect place to begin with students who forget to process text as they read and somehow get to the end with little idea of "what happened." Now we will encourage them along the way to make pictures in their mind, pause to wonder about points that they find unsettling, predict a character's next actions, etc. This is what good readers do (often almost automatically) to understand—and fully enjoy—what they are reading.

COMPREHENSION STRATEGIES THEN AND NOW

Not that long ago, comprehension strategies were like front page news. Previously, though teachers were skilled in supporting students *after* reading (asking plenty of questions about text) and, more recently, had become more proficient in supporting readers *before* reading (activating prior knowledge, setting a purpose, and encouraging predictions), we'd never before seriously considered how we might support readers *during* the reading process itself. The market was soon saturated with books about teaching comprehension strategies.

Many comprehension strategy aficionados believed in teaching one strategy at a time over a long period of time. The problem with this was that the focus was often on the strategies themselves, on "having a strategy": *Can you connect? Can you visualize? Can you question?* As it turned out, kids can apply lots of random strategies as they read and still manage to come away with little knowledge about the text's basic meaning. This was not the approach I advocated in *Constructing Meaning*; I argued for "being strategic," integrating a repertoire of strategies with the focus squarely on using strategies as a vehicle for understanding. In *Constructing Meaning*, the focus is not just on *learning* the strategies, but *using* the strategies. As a reader, can you distinguish between a good opportunity to make a picture in your mind and an opportunity to make a personal connection? More importantly, do all those strategies add up to comprehension of the text?

As the clock ticks on, I'd change almost nothing about my "kid-friendly" approach to teaching students to use comprehension strategies. I have, though, extended my work with strategy applications over the years as teachers have pushed my thinking, asking "What's next?" I've responded with a means of tapping the strategic thinking of more advanced readers as they construct basic meaning (see "Getting Inside the Author's Head" in this chapter), identified applications to deeper strategy use as students reinforce skills and strategies (Chapter Five), and linked comprehension strategies to higher-level thinking through discussion (Chapter Six). I have also thought more seriously about the "connecting" strategy as it seems to cause both teachers and students an undue amount of stress.

BUILDING A BETTER TEXT-TO-SELF CONNECTION

While not exactly a change of perspective, I would speak in a louder voice about the connecting strategy and ask teachers to rethink their instruction regarding text-to-self connections. This is typically the first strategy teachers embrace when they're teaching students to use comprehension strategies (notice it is nearly the first chapter in most strategy instruction books); it should, however, be the *last*. A significant connection to a text is not a coincidental relationship between the reader and some superficial text detail ("The dog in the story looks like my dog…"). A *real* connection addresses the theme and applies that "big idea" to the reader's own life—with an example (or examples) *different from* the details or evidence described by the author.

Take Patricia Polacco's book *Thundercake*. In this story, a little girl is comforted by her grandmother as a thunderstorm approaches. Grandmother and granddaughter make a "thundercake" together to distract the child from the looming storm. What works—and doesn't work—as a connection to this story? Don't tell me that you once made a cake with your grandma; that's a small-detail connection. Don't tell me that your grandma comforts you during thunderstorms, too; that's a copy-cat connection, and I can't tell whether you actually understand the underlying concept or whether this was just a convenient thing for you to say.

What I'm looking for instead is the recognition that readers have connected with the message I expect Polacco was trying to convey: People can help each other when they are upset or worried by showing small kindnesses. Now you tell me about a time (not during a thunderstorm and not about making a cake!) when you were upset and someone did something kind to make you feel better. Or conversely, you could tell me about a time when you showed this same kind of concern for someone else. Note that important connections such as these can't really be made until you've finished the reading. When you ask students to connect too close to the beginning of a text, what you get are connections to background knowledge or inconsequential details because the text's big idea has not become clear yet. Hint: If you teach theme or author's message before teaching about connections, getting good connections from students will be infinitely easier.

A useful update since *Constructing Meaning* was published is the *Making Good Connections* template found in this chapter on page 59 (and on the CD). This encourages students to be metacognitive about the connections they make—without actually writing about their connection every time: What is the *big idea* portrayed by this story? Or if you can't find a connection to the theme: What is the dominant *feeling* that the story expresses? (Focusing on the dominant feeling is a great fallback connection and short-circuits the nearly automatic response from some students: "I don't have any connections to this text…") And finally, what are some small detail or copy-cat connections that don't work for this text? Use this template as a follow-up task for small-group work when students need more reinforcement on the nature of good connections.

Another template intended more for teacher use than student use may be found on page 58 (and on the CD) and helps you identify texts for small-group reading that provide opportunities for using *multiple* strategies. It's likely that there may be a strategy (or two) that are featured in a particular text—which is fine. But if we want students to apply different strategies and develop flexibility in their use, we have to give them texts to read that lead to a variety of different strategy applications.

THE PREQUEL: PART II—TEXT STRUCTURE

While becoming metacognitive about strategy use is essential for the construction of meaning, there's another dimension of basic comprehension that we seldom consider and which holds the key to general understanding about a text: knowledge of text structure. The notion of text structure gets a bit of fanfare when we teach students about informational (non-narrative) text: Is this piece organized as a sequence of events? As cause and effect? As compare/contrast? As main ideas and details? This is useful (though typically under-represented in literacy instruction). But the more basic concern is that identifying text structure is not only relevant to informational (non-narrative) text, but to literary (narrative) text as well. When we ask students to summarize, most often we ask them to summarize a *story*. We think we are teaching this because we are very good at addressing story elements: Who are the characters? What is the problem? What are the roadblocks that keep the problem from being solved right away? What is the solution? How does the story end? But our focus on text elements should not end there.

STORY ELEMENTS OR SEQUENCE OF EVENTS?

It is definitely helpful to teach students about these story elements; in fact, it is essential! But there is another step here that we need to take if we want students to be able to summarize a text after reading it: Is this a problem/solution story—or is it just a sequence of events? There are, of course, other narrative frameworks as well. But, for now, let's focus on the bare essentials, a perfect place to begin for *all* the kids we teach.

My first question when I finish reading a story in any classroom—regardless of the grade: Was this a story that had a problem and a solution? Teach this concept to kids as early as kindergarten as it holds the key to their capacity to summarize. And it's not hard to get this message across, as long as you offer up a broad view of "problem." A problem in a story might be as straightforward as a big, bad wolf who is after some innocent little piggies, or it might be more of an internal conflict, such as the "problem" faced by the main character in *The Raft* by Jim LaMarche. As the story opens, he thinks his grandmother is weird and initially dreads the thought of spending the summer with her in her backwoods cabin. By the end of the story, he has a very different view of Grandma. The critical point here is: Can students find the link between the problem and how the problem/conflict is resolved? On the other hand, maybe there wasn't a resolution to the problem. Or perhaps there wasn't even a problem that needed resolving. Teachers need to direct students' thinking toward this distinction in text structures.

"Which cards will we use to summarize this story?" I ask, a set of "summarizing cards" in each hand. In my left hand: story-part cards (*character, setting, problem…*). In my right hand: sequence cards (*first, next, then…*). When children recognize the structure of a text, they then have a framework to plug in the elements they find in a specific story. Concurrently, they are able to decide for themselves what goes into their summary—and what they should leave out. This resolves the dilemma that frustrates so many teachers: How can I teach them to write summaries that include *enough* information but not *so much* that their summary is more of a complete retelling of the entire story?

Let's let Peter show us how. Peter is the main character in Ezra Jack Keats's beloved story, *Whistle for Willie*. His problem is that he desperately wants to learn to whistle so he can whistle for Willie, his dog. Events in the story directly related to this problem—learning to whistle—belong in a summary; other incidental actions do not.

The story begins, "Oh, how Peter wished he could whistle." Bingo! You think to yourself, "We've only read the first page, and already we have the main character and the problem he faces." You turn the page, expecting to hear about Peter's first failed attempt at whistling. But this is not what happens. Instead, Peter spends the next four pages twirling around and making himself dizzy. This whimsy is very kid like and does much to explain the appeal of Keats's books; it also shows us how important it is for students to have a clear view of the problem in a story and its connection to the resolution. Students who understand this realize that "twirling around" doesn't belong in their summary. Next, Peter finds a large cardboard carton and climbs in—where he tries to whistle incognito. Let's include this in our summary, but we should omit the action on the following pages: drawing a line with chalk to his front door (unrelated to solving the problem). Peter then tries again and again to whistle and ultimately succeeds. In the end, he whistles all the way to the store, Willie by his side. A brief summary of this story might be:

> *A little boy named Peter wanted to learn to whistle so he could call his dog. He kept trying but didn't succeed at first. For example, he hid in a cardboard carton and tried to whistle, and later he tried to act like his dad. In the end, Peter does whistle and his dog follows him all the way to the store.*

You could also create a summary for this story as a series of *events*, though the first event would need to identify the character and problem, and the last (or nearly last) would have to specify the solution. (You still wouldn't include the incidents unrelated to the problem and its solution—unless you're retelling rather than summarizing the story). It's reasonable to say that all problem/solution stories can be summarized as a sequence of events, though the reverse is not true. Many sequence-of-events stories cannot be summarized in terms of story elements.

Take our old friend Alexander (of the no good, very bad day). Alexander's day is a series of calamities, none of which gets resolved before he moves on to the next catastrophe. There is no solution to be found here. This story would need to be summarized with *first, next, then, after that, finally*—or using some variation of these transition words.

Odds are that if you pulled a book from your bookshelf, it would *not* be a problem/solution text—although we've grown up with the myth that most books are "stories" and all stories have a problem and a solution. Consider the following chart.

SUMMARY STRATEGIES, TEXT STRUCTURES, AND POSSIBLE GENRES

Summary Strategy	Text Structure	Possible Genres
Story parts	Problem/ solution	• Realistic fiction • Fairytales • Folk tales • Myths & legends • Historical fiction • Mysteries • Adventure stories
First, next, then...	Sequence of events	• Personal narratives • Biographies • Journal or "letter" texts • Chapters from a chapter book • How-to books • Life-cycle books • Narrative nonfiction
Main idea/details	Expository	• "All about" books • Essay • Most content-area materials with headings/subheadings
Other More Advanced Summary Strategies, Text Structures, and Genres		
Point/ counterpoint	Compare/ contrast	• Letters to the editor (two points of view) • Story told from two or more perspectives
If...then	Cause/effect	• Advertisement
Representative examples	Description	• Travel brochure
Who, what, when...	News event	• Newspaper article

One of the interesting observations you might make from this chart is that while we have this image in our mind that the literary world is full of texts with problems and solutions (like your garden-variety sitcom), there are far fewer genres that can be summarized using this structure than those that can be summarized in other ways.

Reading a text and deciding on its structure is a new way of looking at reading for many teachers. When I do workshops on constructing meaning and distribute books to teachers so they can examine them for their structure, I am always amazed by the thoughtful conversation this generates.

"Would you summarize this one as problem/solution or as a series of events?" This teacher was pondering *Miss Rumphius* (Barbara Cooney). "At first, I thought it must be problem/solution because Miss Rumphius is given a challenge when she's a little girl to make the world a more beautiful place. And at the end, she plants all those lupines to respond to that challenge. But the whole middle of the book has nothing to do with solving the problem; it's more like a biography. So I think my kids would have an easier time seeing this as a series of events."

Looking at books through a structural lens also alerts teachers to nuances of particular texts that need to be considered when they use them for summarizing in their classrooms.

"Hey, look at this," one teacher pointed out. "This book has more of a *setup* than a *setting*. The entire first half of the book is about Kenya before the land was ravaged. And the problem isn't even introduced until midway through the story" (*Planting the Trees of Kenya* by Wangari Maathai).

Another discovery: "In this story, you don't really need to tell about the setting because the events could happen anywhere." (Many realistic-fiction stories contain a *backdrop* rather than an *integral* setting.)

"What do I do with this one?" a primary teacher asked. "It's very cute, but it's just a bunch of examples illustrating a theme." (The story was *Not All Princesses Dress in Pink* by Jane Yolen; "Don't try to summarize that one," was my suggestion.)

On page 57, I provide a template, *Texts to Use for Summarizing* (with a couple of samples filled in), to help you think through the texts you choose for summarizing. This chart is blank on the CD, ready for you to fill in yourself.

This puts into perspective the instructional practices that follow for constructing basic meaning about a text. I offer five formats—along with all the resources you will need to focus your teaching for each one. The formats include: **Story Elements, Sequence of Events, Main Idea and Details, Comprehension Strategies (Basic),** and **Comprehension Strategies (Advanced)**. How do you decide whether to ask students to construct meaning using the comprehension strategies or by addressing text elements directly? It's your call. Both will lead to the same outcome—the capacity to summarize. If the text offers opportunities to apply a variety of comprehension strategies, I often focus on strategies. If the text presents clearly defined narrative or non-narrative text elements or an obvious sequence, I generally organize my teaching around those. Remember that not all students will need this small-group "prequel" to other instructional focuses. But many students will need this much of the time.

QUESTIONS TO CONSIDER

1. Do you regularly include comprehension strategy instruction as a feature of your literacy curriculum? If so, what goes well? What goes not so well?

2. What are the problems your students typically encounter with summarizing?

3. Do you often have students who have difficulty constructing basic meaning about a text? What do you think is responsible for this problem?

4. What questions do you hope the remainder of this chapter will answer for you?

TEXTS TO USE FOR SUMMARIZING

Text	Genre/Structure	How to Summarize	Special Text Features
A River Ran Wild by Lynne Cherry	Historical fiction	Sequence of events	Limit the number of events to be included
The Honest-to-Goodness Truth by Patricia McKissack	Realistic fiction	Problem/solution	Clearly structured story

TEXTS TO USE FOR APPLYING COMPREHENSION STRATEGIES

	FEATURED COMPREHENSION STRATEGIES					
TEXT	**Noticing**	**Picturing**	**Wondering**	**Predicting**	**Figuring Out**	**Connecting**

MAKING GOOD CONNECTIONS

TEXT	GOOD CONNECTIONS		POOR CONNECTIONS
	Theme/Big Idea	**Feelings**	**Copy-cat/Small Detail**

INSTRUCTIONAL FOCUS: COMPREHENSION STRATEGIES (BASIC)

What's the purpose?

The purpose of this instructional focus is for students to interact with text using a repertoire of comprehension strategies in order to construct basic meaning about a text. The strategies are intended to be a vehicle for improved comprehension, not just an opportunity for applying random strategies. These strategies give students the language they need to talk about text, thus helping them engage in authentic conversations about what they read.

Who would benefit from this focus?

This is a very low-risk instructional approach since students make meaning in any way that works for them; the teacher does not pose directed questions that students must answer. Thus, this is a great focus for students who are typically reluctant to participate for fear of being "wrong." Children of varying ages and skill levels enjoy this focus and succeed with it even when they have not had extensive training in the use of comprehension strategies; they learn more about the strategies as they apply them. Providing students with an opportunity to work with strategies in this way is a good small-group instructional focus for *all* students about once (or even twice) a week as it serves as a healthy reminder that using comprehension strategies can do much to help us understand what we read.

What kinds of texts should I use?

Both fiction and nonfiction texts as well as poetry may be used effectively for this instructional focus. While short text is always perfect for small-group instruction, chapters from chapter books or excerpts from longer texts can also support basic strategy use. Teachers should choose texts that provide students with opportunities to apply a range of strategies. Rich texts with beautiful language will generate powerful <u>pictures</u> in students' minds. Realistic fiction leads to meaningful <u>connections</u>. Texts centered on moral dilemmas, such as civil rights and the Holocaust, cause children to ask important <u>questions and</u> wonder. Adventure stories beg for <u>predictions</u>. Stories that *show* rather than *tell* require students to <u>notice</u>. Texts with an important message encourage children to <u>figure out</u> the theme or lesson.

What resources will I need for teaching and assessing?

- *Strategy Cue Cards* (I use two laminated sets of the cards for the group so more than one student can choose a particular strategy), page 62
- *Active Reader Report* (follow-up strategy activity for intermediate students), page 63
- *Strategy Exit Slip* (follow-up strategy activity for primary students or struggling readers), page 64
- **Other Strategy Follow-up Activities** (see pages 153-197 in *Constructing Meaning*)
- *Comprehension Strategy Checklist* (for students' self-reflection), page 66
- *Comprehension Strategy Rubric* (for the teacher to assess students), page 65

How do I implement this?

1. Place two sets of the strategy cue cards on the table so all students can reach them.

2. Remind students that the strategy card they choose should help them understand the text more deeply.

3. Identify a chunk of text for students to read, mindful of students' reading skills. (More capable readers should read longer chunks; beginning and struggling readers should read chunks that are quite short—a few lines to a few paragraphs.)

4. Instruct students to read the first chunk of text and choose <u>one</u> strategy that helped them understand or think more deeply about this part of the text.

5. After all students have read the text chunk and picked up a cue card, the teacher asks students to discuss the strategy they chose. The goal is for students to build on each other's ideas in the manner of a true "book club" experience. This will not be automatic at first but should be a goal of small-group instruction when the focus is using these metacognitive strategies. The teacher should intervene to ask students to "prove it in the text" by reading portions of the text aloud that contain the necessary evidence.

6. After the first chunk of text has been discussed via the comprehension strategies, cue cards should be placed back in the center of the table and the session should proceed in the same manner with subsequent chunks of text. Finishing the text is less important than exploring students' strategic thinking as they read, so it is okay not to complete even a relatively short text in a single session. Additionally, as students become more competent strategy users, the length of the text chunk should be increased to give them the opportunity for more internal monitoring of their thinking.

7. By the time students have completed the text, they should have a command of text elements as the intent of using these strategies is to facilitate basic construction of meaning. The teacher should check this: What was the problem and how was it solved? What is the main idea and which details support it?

8. Students can be asked to complete a follow-up task, such as the *Strategy Exit Slip* or *Active Reader Report*, to reflect one more time on their strategy use.

How do I measure students' success?

Any follow-up task that requires students to demonstrate basic construction of meaning will let you know whether the comprehension strategies have been effective in helping them monitor their thinking. Observation of students during the group session using criteria on the *Rubric for Assessing a Student's Use of Comprehension Strategies* will allow you to analyze students' use of strategies based on important criteria. Students can use the *Comprehension Strategy Checklist* to reflect on their own strategy use.

- **Level 1:** Accurate construction of meaning based on active strategy use

- **Level 2:** Accurate and insightful construction of meaning based on active strategy use

Connecting	Predicting
Picturing	Noticing
Wondering	Figuring Out

NAME: _____   **DATE:** _____

Noticing

Notice a place you stopped to think about your thinking. Why was this a good place to pause and think? What detail did you notice?

Picturing

Find a place where the author has described something so you can picture it in your mind. What do you picture?

Wondering

What is something you wondered about as you read this text (or part of the text)?

Predicting

Where did you make a prediction about something that might happen next (or something you might learn)?

Figuring Out

What did you figure out that the author didn't tell you directly?

Connecting

Was it easy or difficult to connect to this text (or part of the text)? Why?

STRATEGY EXIT SLIP

Name: _____ Date: _____

One strategy I used today to help me understand this text is:

Connecting   **Wondering**   **Picturing**

Predicting   **Noticing**   **Figuring Out**

Here's a place in the text where I used this strategy:

_____

_____

_____

STRATEGY EXIT SLIP

Name: _____ Date: _____

One strategy I used today to help me understand this text is:

Connecting   **Wondering**   **Picturing**

Predicting   **Noticing**   **Figuring Out**

Here's a place in the text where I used this strategy:

_____

_____

_____

STRATEGY EXIT SLIP

Name: _____ Date: _____

One strategy I used today to help me understand this text is:

Connecting   **Wondering**   **Picturing**

Predicting   **Noticing**   **Figuring Out**

Here's a place in the text where I used this strategy:

_____

_____

_____

RUBRIC FOR ASSESSING A STUDENT'S USE OF COMPREHENSION STRATEGIES

STUDENT'S NAME: _____   GRADE: _____   DATE: _____

	Excellent = 2	Developing = 1	Needs attention = 0
Accurate use of strategies	Uses comprehension strategies accurately almost all of the time to probe deep meaning of text	Generally uses comprehension strategies accurately; strategies may sometimes be mislabeled or some strategy applications may be superficial	Strategy applications are often inaccurate and/or superficial
Flexible use of strategies	Uses a varied repertoire of strategies and recognizes when a particular strategy could be especially helpful in constructing meaning	Tends to rely on a few "favorite" strategies and doesn't seem to see the relative merits of one strategy over another in particular situations	Seems to feel comfortable with only one or two strategies and relies on them even when they are not relevant
Use of strategies to construct meaning	There is a clear link between the use of comprehension strategies and good comprehension of text, often with direct reference to one or more strategies	Use of comprehension strategies sometimes results in improved comprehension, though this improvement generally occurs just within literal-level thinking about text	Comprehension remains poor despite instructional focus on comprehension strategies
Active engagement in strategy use	Initiates use of strategies without prompting or modeling; actively uses strategies during both group discussions and independent reading	Uses strategies willingly during group and independent work but sometimes needs prompting	Seldom uses strategies without specific teacher prompting or modeling

NOTES ABOUT THIS STUDENT:

Accurate use of strategies:

_____

Flexible use of strategies:

_____

Use of strategies to construct meaning:

_____

Active engagement in strategy use:

_____

NAME: _____   **DATE:** _____

_____ **I use each strategy <u>correctly</u> as I read.** (I know the meaning of all six comprehension strategies.)

_____ **I use <u>different strategies</u> at *different times* during my reading.** (Is this a good time to make a picture in my mind? Is this a good time to make a connection? Etc.)

_____ **I use my strategies to help me <u>understand what I am reading</u>.** (I can explain how one of my strategies improved my comprehension.)

_____ **I <u>think about and talk about strategies</u> in my own reading, even without my teacher's help.** (I can do this during a discussion and when I'm reading on my own.)

INSTRUCTIONAL FOCUS:
COMPREHENSION STRATEGIES (ADVANCED)

What's the purpose?

The purpose of this focus is to give competent strategy users practice using metacognitive strategies at a slightly higher level in order to construct basic meaning. The usual format for strategy use (strategy cue cards displayed on your small-group instruction table for students to pick up as they read) remains a valuable technique for children to initially learn about the strategies and practice using them. But strong readers can be pushed to go deeper—right from the beginning. This focus asks students to "get inside the author's head." This does not mean that we want students to find one "correct" meaning for a text, but that we want them to think more seriously about *how* they view a text as a well-crafted piece of writing.

Who would benefit from this focus?

This focus would be a wonderful next step for students who have already learned about comprehension strategies via the basic cue-cards-on-the-table format and who are adept at basic strategy use. It would also be beneficial for older students who are capable of thinking more abstractly.

What kinds of texts should I use?

Well-crafted text is essential in order for this focus to be successful. The text needs beautiful language with rich imagery, a significant message with the possibility of multiple interpretations, opportunities for personal connections, and enough ambiguity to keep the reader questioning. Poems are perfect for this—not the fun variety by Shel Silverstein and Jack Prelutsky, but more thoughtful works by Emily Dickinson and Robert Frost, among others of course. Cynthia Rylant's little anthology of short stories featuring animals, *Every Living Thing*, is great for studying short fiction. Letters to the editor provide experience with point of view and help students find their own voice in thinking and talking about real-life issues. Individual chapters from a novel work well, too.

What resources will I need for teaching and assessing?

- *Getting Inside the Author's Head Focus Sheet* (copied on card stock for all students in the group), page 69
- *Getting Inside the Author's Head: Tips for the Peer Leader* (for use when a peer leader facilitates the discussion instead of the classroom teacher), page 70
- *Active Reader Report for "Getting Inside the Author's Head"* (follow-up strategy activity for more advanced readers), page 71
- *Comprehension Strategy Checklist for Advanced Readers* (for student self-reflection), page 73
- *Comprehension Strategy Rubric for Advanced Readers* (for teachers to assess students), page 72

How do I implement this?

1. Determine with students where to pause within the text to reflect on their strategic thinking. Because this small-group focus is intended for more advanced readers, the portions of text should be longer than those of other small-group approaches to constructing basic meaning.

Also, right from the beginning, students should be part of the "decision-making team" to determine where in the text they will pause and reflect. Knowing when to stop to take stock of what you've read so far is an important skill for effective reading: "Look at the length of this text. How many times should we pause? Where should we pause?" (These pausing points can be flagged with a sticky note as a reminder to students.)

2. Ask students to read the first chunk of text and review their strategy sheet to determine particular strategies that helped them "get inside the author's head": "What do you think the author wanted us to think about in this part of the text? Were there points you think the author wanted us to question? Are you inspired to picture any words, phrases, or passages in this portion of the text?" The teacher should always be prepared to share his own strategy thinking as a model or simply as another member of the group. But the real goal is to get students to initiate conversation points themselves and to build on each other's ideas.

3. After the first chunk of text has been explored, students should read the next chunk, following the same basic procedure.

4. At the completion of the reading (which may take more than one group session), students should be asked to briefly summarize the entire text to make sure their strategy use did, in fact, lead to basic construction of meaning.

5. There are variations of this instructional focus that teachers might also want to consider:

   a. **Invite a "peer leader" to facilitate the group.** Lots of students love the opportunity to "play teacher," and some are amazingly good at this. Remember, though, that leading the group for this instructional focus does not mean mechanically reading strategy prompts off the strategy sheet. The role of the peer leader (similar to the role of the teacher for this instructional focus) would be to facilitate give and take among all members of the group to construct meaning collaboratively. Use the resource *Getting Inside the Author's Head: Tips for the Peer Leader* (page 70) for guidance in the effective implementation of this variation.

   b. **Begin the process in the group and send students back to their seats to read the remainder of the text (or a designated portion)—with a follow-up discussion around the strategies the next day.** This works well with longer texts and for students who are capable of getting to meaning with limited teacher guidance

How do I measure students' success?

The *Active Reader Report for Advanced Readers* (page 71) or any other means of documenting students' successful construction of meaning via strategy application would be an appropriate way of measuring their success. Perhaps the best method of evaluation for this instructional focus would be through the discussion itself. The *Rubric for Assessing Advanced Students' Use of Comprehension Strategies* (page 72) should be used to identify particular criteria. Students should also assess their own success by using the *Comprehension Strategy Checklist for Advanced Readers* (page 73).

- **Level 1:** Evidence of strategy use that led students to an accurate understanding of the text, although comprehension may be more literal than critical.

- **Level 2:** Evidence of deep understanding of the text generated from the capacity to view it as a well-crafted piece of writing open to personal interpretation.

What details did you **notice** that you considered especially helpful in understanding this text? Did any details foreshadow events later in the text?

What part(s) of the text do you think the author wanted us to **picture** in our mind? What did the author do to help us get this mental picture?

What do you think the author wanted us to **wonder** about *before* reading this text? *During* reading? *After* reading?

Where in this text do you think the author wanted us to **predict**?

Can you **figure out** why the author might have written this text? What did s/he want us to think about?

What do you think is the **connection** that the author wanted us to make to this text? How could this connection make a difference in the way we live our lives?

GETTING INSIDE THE AUTHOR'S HEAD: TIPS FOR THE PEER LEADER

- With other students in the group, decide on good stopping points as you read so that everyone can monitor their understanding.

- Ask students to cover up the parts of the text they haven't read yet so that they don't read ahead.

- Ask students to make some **predictions** before reading based on the genre and title—and maybe the author if it's someone you know. Also think about what the author wanted you to **wonder** about.

- Ask students to read the first chunk of text and to refer to their strategy sheet for *Getting Inside the Author's Head*. They should have a strategy point to share after reading this part of the text.

- When everyone has finished the first chunk, invite students to share their thinking.

- If no one volunteers, you can start the discussion with something like: "Did anyone find a place where the author…?"

- Always follow up on your classmates' answers by asking "Why?" or "What made you say that?" (That will get kids to go back to the text to "prove it.")

- After one student has shared, ask "Does anyone have anything to add?" or "Does anyone have a different opinion?"

- Good ways to get into the author's head DURING each chunk include:
    - **Noticing** details that you consider important;
    - **Picturing** something (and thinking about what the author did to give you a good mental picture);
    - **Wondering** about something that is confusing or unsettling; and
    - **Predicting** what will happen next.

- Save **figuring out** the message for AFTER you read.

- After figuring out the message, get students to talk about their **connection** to this big idea—and you can even think about an "action step" based on this connection. (How could your connection change the way you act in a particular situation?)

ACTIVE READER REPORT FOR "GETTING INSIDE THE AUTHOR'S HEAD"

NAME: _____ DATE: _____

Noticing	**Picturing**
Notice a small detail where the author *shows* rather than *tells*	Find a place where you can **picture** what the author is talking about. What has the author done to help you get this picture in your mind?
Wondering	**Predicting**
What do you think the author wants you to **wonder** about as you read this text? (You can consider *before*, *during*, and *after* reading.)	Where does the author "leave you hanging," causing you to **predict** what might happen next?
Figuring Out	**Connecting**
Did you **figure out** the author's message in this text? What did the author want readers to think about?	Can you apply the author's message by **connecting** it to your own life?

RUBRIC FOR ASSESSING ADVANCED STUDENTS' USE OF COMPREHENSION STRATEGIES

STUDENT'S NAME: _____ **GRADE:** _____ **DATE:** _____

	Excellent = 2	Developing = 1	Needs attention = 0
Noticing	Notices specific details that are significant to the text and contribute to deeper understanding	Notices some details that contribute to meaning but misses other key points	Does not read closely enough to identify important details—leading to only a general understanding of the text
Picturing	Uses multiple senses to create mental images of the author's words; able to elaborate on imagery to enhance visual imagery	Able to recognize words in the text that contribute to visual imagery; able to describe the mental picture	Very limited ability to detect imagery in a text; may lack sufficient vocabulary or background knowledge to picture the author's words
Wondering	Asks probing questions that explore key ideas or themes in a text	Asks questions that show understanding of basic text elements, though the focus may be more literal than inferential	Does not ask questions, or the questions may not be relevant to the text
Predicting	Predictions are based on a deep understanding of the characters' motives or other key concepts within the text	Predictions are logical based on clear evidence from the text	Predictions rely more on background knowledge than textual evidence, or the predictions just don't make sense
Figuring Out	Independently infers and synthesizes information from the text in order to achieve deeper understanding	Infers and synthesizes information from the text to achieve deeper understanding with some support from the teacher	Unable to infer or synthesize to move beyond literal understanding, even with much teacher support
Connecting	Makes personal or text connections to the theme or "big idea" of the text with meaningful personal examples	Makes personal or text connections to the theme or "big idea" of the text, but the examples could use more elaboration	Makes connections based on small details that do not contribute to comprehension, or the examples "copy" those of the author

NOTES ABOUT THIS STUDENT:

Greatest area of strength:

_____

Greatest area of need:

_____

COMPREHENSION STRATEGY CHECKLIST FOR ADVANCED READERS

NAME: _____ **DATE:** _____

TEXT: _____

_____ I **noticed** lots of details in this text that helped me to understand it more deeply.

_____ I **pictured** many parts of this text using different senses and could imagine these scenes vividly in my mind.

_____ I **wondered** about lots of things as I read this text that caused me to think about its meaning more deeply.

_____ I **predicted** the outcome of particular situations in this text by carefully considering all the text evidence I'd discovered so far.

_____ I **figured out** the message of this text on my own without my teacher or someone else explaining it to me.

_____ I **connected** to the big idea of this text with meaningful personal examples.

INSTRUCTIONAL FOCUS: STORY ELEMENTS

What's the purpose?

The purpose of this instructional focus is for students to identify basic story elements in a text with a traditional problem-solution structure. As they read, students should look for and identify **characters, setting, problem, complications that prevent the immediate solution of the problem, solution,** and **extended ending**. At the conclusion of the lesson, struggling and beginning readers may only be able to identify individual story elements when prompted by the teacher. More capable readers should be able to <u>retell</u> or <u>summarize</u> the story independently.

Who would benefit from this focus?

This is a useful small-group focus for students of any grade level who may not attain a general understanding about a narrative text on their own. Identification of basic story elements is a prerequisite for success with virtually all other comprehension objectives. This focus would also be helpful to primary students who are just beginning their exploration of reading comprehension as well as English learners who need to become familiar with academic vocabulary to talk about the stories they read (characters, setting, problem, etc.).

What kinds of texts should I use?

The *only* texts that will work for this activity are texts with a problem-solution format. For young or struggling readers, choose very simple stories with a clear plot line. *All* story elements should be present. Be careful not to choose a text that is a "personal narrative" showing a sequence of events with no real problem or conflict. Most texts for this instructional focus will be fiction—unless it is an account of a real-life problem solved by a real person. Additionally, *short* text is preferable to longer text as it can be read during a single session, facilitating students' retention of meaning.

What resources will I need for teaching and assessing?

- *Story Part Cue Cards* (one laminated set for the whole group, page 76) or *Story Part Detective Card* (one card for each student in the group), page 77
- *Story Part Chart* (enlarged and laminated for use in the group or individual chart for each group member), page 78
- *Answer Frame for Summarizing a Story: A3-a* (to get students started on the process of written response), page 79
- *Answer Frame for Summarizing a Story: Alternate Summary Form* (suitable for more advanced summary that synthesizes story elements), page 80
- *Student Checklist for Retelling* (for student self-reflection), page 82
- *Student Checklist for Summarizing* (for student self-reflection), page 84
- *Summarizing Rubric* (for the teacher to assess students' summarizing), page 83
- *Retelling Rubric* (for the teacher to assess students' retelling), page 81

How do I implement this?

1. Place *Story Part Cue Cards* on the table so that all students can reach them.

2. Remind students where to *usually* look for various story elements within a text (at the beginning—characters, setting, problem; in the middle—complications; at the end—solution and ending).

3. Identify a chunk of text for students to read, being mindful of students' reading skills. (More capable readers should read longer chunks; beginning and struggling readers should read chunks that are quite short—a few lines to a few paragraphs.)

4. Instruct students to read the first chunk of text. Anyone finding a story element may pick up the corresponding *Story Part Cue Card*.

5. After all students have read the text chunk and picked up relevant *Story Part Cue Cards*, the teacher asks students to discuss the elements they found, guiding and supporting as needed by probing and extending their thinking: "What did you find out about this character? How did the setting change on this page?" Etc. The teacher should also ask students to "prove it in the text" by reading portions of the story aloud that contain the necessary evidence.

6. After the first text chunk has been read and discussed, the teacher instructs students to read the next chunk using the same process.

7. After reading each chunk, the teacher may chart story elements on the enlarged *Story Part Chart*. Or, the teacher can review orally the new information after each chunk, adding it to what has been learned previously about the story.

8. At the end of the text, the teacher should ask students to identify all story elements. These may be synthesized into an oral retelling or an oral or a written summary based on students' developmental level. Written assessment (if used at all) should be completed independently *after* the group has met—not during group time—unless your group is particularly low.

9. As an alternative to using the *Story Part Cue Cards*, students can each have a *Story Part Detective Card* to mark story elements as they find them. Use poker chips, dried beans, or whatever for markers.

How do I measure students' success?

Accurate identification of all story elements in an appropriate format:

Level 1: Oral identification of individual story elements when prompted by the teacher

Level 2: Oral retelling of the story looking back at the text

Level 3: Oral retelling of the story without looking back at the text

Level 4: Written summary that is more of a "written retell" briefly specifying all story elements

Level 5: Written summary that synthesizes story elements, capturing the gist of the text in just a few sentences

Level 6: Written summary that synthesizes story elements and also incorporates the theme or "big idea"

Characters

Setting

Problem

Trying to solve the problem: 1

Trying to solve the problem: 2

Trying to solve the problem: 3

The solution

The ending

	Characters
	Setting
	Problem
	Trying to solve the problem
	Solution
	Ending

STORY PART CHART

NAME: _____ **DATE:** _____

TEXT: _____

Important characters

The setting (if it is important)

The problem (the situation that gets the action started)

A couple of important things that happen in the middle of the story

---

How the problem gets solved

How the story ends (if something happens after the problem gets solved)

A3-a: Briefly summarize this story.

<u>Strategy for reading</u>

Think about all of the different parts of a story: characters, setting, problem, events, solution, ending. At the beginning of a story, look for places that the author is telling you about the characters, the setting, and the problem. In the middle of the story, look for events or places where the characters are trying to solve the problem. (Look for important events.) At the end of the story, look for the solution to the problem.

<u>Strategy for writing</u>

1. Tell the main character, setting, and problem.
2. Tell 2 or 3 things that happen before the problem gets solved.
3. Tell how the problem gets solved and what happens at the very end.

The main character in this story is _____

The story takes place _____

The problem that gets the story going is_____

_____

Something that happens before the problem gets solved is

_____

_____

Something else that happens before the problem gets solved is

_____

_____

The problem gets solved by

_____

_____

Here is how the story ends:

_____

_____

A3-a: Briefly summarize this story.

Reading strategy for summarizing
Make sure you find all of the story parts: main characters, setting, problem, important events, solution, how the story ends.

Writing strategy for summarizing
1. Tell what happens at the <u>beginning</u>. (Talk about the main character and the problem—and the setting if it is important.)

2. Tell what happens in the <u>middle</u>. (Talk about one or two important things that happened on the way to solving the problem.)

3. Tell what happens at the <u>end</u>. (Talk about how the problem gets solved and how the story ends.)

At the beginning of the story, _____

_____

_____

_____

_____

Then, _____

_____

_____

_____

_____

_____

_____

At the end, _____

_____

_____

_____

_____

_____

 **STORY RETELLING RUBRIC**

NAME: _____ DATE: _____

TEXT: _____

Element	High Quality (2)	Developing (1)	Needs Attention (0)
Characters	Your retelling told about the characters so others had a good idea of what they are like.	Your retelling named the characters, but did not tell too much about them.	Your retelling confused the characters or did not name them.
Setting	Your retelling helps others get a clear picture in their head of when and where the story took place.	Your retelling gave some general details about where and when the story took place.	Your retelling did not describe when and where the story took place so the reader could "picture it."
Problem	Your retelling told what the problem was and how it might be solved.	Your retelling included part of the problem but was incomplete.	Your retelling did not tell what's the matter in this story. What problem are the characters trying to solve?
Solution	Your retelling told what the characters did to solve the problem.	Your retelling included events from the end of the story but didn't indicate what contributed to the solution.	Your retelling left out major events including how the problem got solved.
Delivery	You used good rhythm and gestures. There was expression in your voice. Your voice changed for different characters.	Your rhythm and expression were good most of the time. You used some gestures. Your voice changed for most of the characters.	Your rhythm and expression need improving. You need to use gestures. Your voice should change for different characters.

Student's greatest strengths: _____

_____

_____

Area(s) of need: _____

_____

_____

NAME: _____ DATE: _____

In my retelling:

____ I told about the characters so someone could imagine
what they are like.

____ I told about the setting so someone could get a good picture
in their head of when and where the story took place.

____ I told about the problem so someone could see that this
was a bad situation.

____ I told about all of the things that happened in the story
before the problem got solved using lots of details.

____ I told what happened to solve the problem.

____ I used good expression and even some gestures to
retell the story.

 **STORY SUMMARY RUBRIC**

NAME: _____ DATE: _____

TEXT: _____

Element	High Quality (2)	Developing (1)	Needs Attention (0)
Story elements	Your summary included all important story parts: characters, setting, problem, key events, and solution.	Your summary included all story parts but was too long or included too few details.	Your summary included information about the story that was incorrect, or many elements of the story were missing.
Sequence	Your summary included story events in the order in which they occurred in the text.	Your summary was stated in a mostly logical manner but could have been presented more clearly.	Your summary seemed to be a list of unrelated details.
Important points	Your summary clearly identified the parts of the story that were *most* important.	Your summary identified important points in the story, but also included some points that were less important.	Your summary focused mostly on little details that really weren't that important.
Length	Your summary was just the right length—not too long and not too short.	Your summary is a bit too long or not quite long enough. Do you have too many details? Not enough information?	Your summary is much too long—nearly as long as the story itself. Or, it is much too short (just a sentence or two).
Paraphrasing	You have stated information in your own words and have shown that you really understood what you read.	Most of your summary is in your own words, but you seem a little confused about some of the meaning.	You mostly copied words right out of the story. You don't seem to understand the story or what you wrote.
Writing quality	Your summary was easy to read and showed good attention to spelling, punctuation, capitalization, and grammar.	Your summary showed some attention to spelling, punctuation, capitalization, and grammar. Please proofread to catch your errors.	Your summary had many written language errors. Let's work on this together.

Student's greatest strengths: _____

_____

_____

Area(s) of need: _____

_____

_____

NAME: _____ **DATE:** _____

In my summary:

____ I included all story elements: characters, setting, problem, important events, and solution.

____ I put story events in the correct order.

____ I identified only the parts of the story that were the *most* important.

____ I made sure my summary was a good length—not too long and not too short.

____ I wrote the summary in my own words, showing that I understood what I read.

____ I paid attention to spelling, capital letters, and punctuation.

INSTRUCTIONAL FOCUS: SEQUENCE OF EVENTS

What's the purpose?

The purpose of this instructional focus is for students to construct basic meaning about a fiction or nonfiction text when the format is not problem/solution for narrative or main idea/detail for nonfiction. We tend to think that all "stories" contain a problem and progress toward a solution and that nonfiction is simply organized around main ideas and details—but that is not the case. Personal narratives or memoirs are typically snapshots of a moment in time—a birthday party, a day at the beach, a backyard picnic—where the author describes a sequence of events from the beginning of the experience to the end; there is no particular "problem" that needs to be solved. (Sometimes we call these "bed-to-bed" stories.) When the sequence is someone's life story (birth-to-death), that's a biography. The story may be fiction or nonfiction. An author of a nonfiction piece who takes information about an animal's life, for instance, and converts it to a life-cycle story instead of just delivering information in an expository fashion is also writing a text that is a narrative where the essential structure is a sequence of events. Likewise, a "how-to" book (example: *How a House Is Built* by Gail Gibbons) may be summarized as a sequence of steps. The purpose of this instructional focus is for students to both recognize this sequence and be able to summarize a text using this *first, next, then…*format.

Who would benefit from this focus?

All students need exposure to this alternative summary structure because it characterizes many texts; readers should be able to recognize it when they see it and summarize accordingly. This format can be introduced in the primary grades as there are many leveled texts—both fiction and nonfiction—suitable for summarizing in this sequential manner. As readers become more competent, they should determine for themselves whether a text is problem/solution, main idea/details, or a sequence of events or steps.

What kinds of texts should I use?

For this sequential focus, look for biographies or partial biographies (a portion of a person's life), personal narratives or memoirs that describe a special event, narrative nonfiction about the life of an animal, and how-to books.

What resources will I need for teaching and assessing?

- *Sequence Cue Cards* (one set for the whole group), page 88
- *Answer Frame for Summarizing a Sequence of Events or Steps in a Process*: A3-b (to get students started on the process of written response), page 89
- *Sequencing Rubric* (for teachers to assess students' ability to summarize by sequencing events or steps in a text that is not problem/solution or main idea/details), page 90
- *Sequencing Checklist* (for students to reflect on their own ability to summarize using a sequence of events or steps in a process), page 91

How do I implement this?

1. Place *Sequence Cue Cards* on the table where all students can reach them.

2. For students just beginning to work with fiction text that does not contain a problem and a solution, or nonfiction that is essentially a chain of events or steps in a process, explain that some stories are more like an adventure or just a description of an experience; sometimes there is not a problem that needs to be solved. Similarly, some nonfiction text is not organized by a main idea and details but is just a series of events or steps in a process.

3. Talk about the kinds of texts that fall into this category and show students some examples (personal narrative: *Alexander and the Terrible, Horrible, No Good, Very Bad Day* by Judith Viorst; any biography; a how-to book such as *How a House Is Built* by Gail Gibbons; a nonfiction narrative like *One Tiny Turtle* by Nicola Davies).

4. Explain to students that the text they read today will not be summarized in the "usual" way using story parts or main idea and details. Today's story will be summarized by identifying the main events of the text in order. Discuss the transition words you can use to summarize a sequence of events (*first, next, then, after that, finally*). Be sure to mention that these words (other than *first* and *finally*) don't need to occur in any particular sequence and that there can be more events—or fewer—than indicated by the five cards on the table. All events selected for summarizing, however, should be *important* events. I find it useful to give students an approximate number of points to include: *Look for three or four events to include in the summary of this text*. Or: *You shouldn't need more than five events when you summarize today's text.*

5. Read the first chunk of text together. Using a sticky note or some other means of identifying something students think might be important, ask them to mark an important point if they think they find one.

6. Discuss the points students highlighted and instruct them to use this same process throughout the remainder of the text to find other potential points to include in their summary. The reading can be done during the group session if students' thinking needs to be monitored. Or, they can return to their seats to complete the task independently if they are capable of doing so.

7. Tell students that after they've highlighted all of the potential points to include in their summary, they should review them to refine their choices: Do they have too many points? (Which ones can they eliminate?) Do they have too few points, making it hard for someone to get an idea of what this text was really about? Should other points be added? (Re-read to find other key ideas to include.)

8. As their final step, students can create a written sequential summary using the *Answer Frame for Summarizing a Sequence of Events or Steps in a Process*. It might be helpful to some students to come back to the group first to share their summary points orally before responding in writing.

How do I measure students' success?

The foremost criterion in assessing students' capacity to create a sequential summary should be their ability to distinguish important from unimportant events in the text (big ideas rather than small details). When students meet this criterion, their level of proficiency can be measured as follows:

Level 1: Oral identification of individual important events or steps in a process when prompted by the teacher

Level 2: Oral identification of all important events or steps in a process without teacher prompting

Level 3: Written sequential summary completed with some teacher support; may use answer frame

Level 4: Written sequential summary completed independently; no teacher support; no answer frame

First

Next

Then

After that

Finally

A3-b: Summarize the main things that happened in this [book] in order.

Strategy for reading

Think about the different things that happen in this [book]. What happens first? What happens next? Does something else happen? What happens at the very end? Try to keep track of the important things that happen. Try to remember them in order.

Strategy for writing

1. Tell what happens *first*.
2. Tell what happens *next*.
3. Tell what happens *after that*.
4. Tell what happens *at the end*.

The first thing that happens is _____

_____

_____

Next, _____

_____

_____

Then, _____

_____

_____

After that, _____

_____

_____

Finally, _____

_____

_____

RUBRIC FOR SEQUENTIAL SUMMARY

	High quality (2)	Developing (1)	Needs attention (0)
Number of relevant points included	There is an appropriate number of events included in the sequence for the length of the text; points included are significant—not just small details	The student included a few too many or too few points; there is a mix of important points and small details	The student basically retold the entire text or the summary is too sparse to be considered a summary; unable to distinguish main points from small details
Chronology	The summary shows a clear and accurate chronology with good use of transition words; you get a good sense of this text	The events are basically sequential but leave the reader a bit confused about the process; some transition words used	The chronology is inaccurate; very difficult to piece together the process; no sense of transition
Details	There is sufficient detail to explain each point but not too much detail	There is either too much elaboration of details or not enough	Details are inaccurate, missing, or irrelevant
Synthesis	The student explicitly indicates how this sequence of events or steps in a process contributes to overall meaning (theme, big idea, etc.)	The summary implies that the student understands the overall significance of the events, but there is no direct statement	There is no indication that the student understands how all of the steps or events fit together to create a message

Strengths: _____

_____

_____

Needs: _____

_____

_____

MY SEQUENCE SUMMARY CHECKLIST

NAME: _____ DATE: _____

TEXT: _____

_____   I have included just the right **number of events** or steps in my summary—not too many and not too few.

_____   The **order of events** or steps in my summary is clear. I used transition words.

_____   My summary includes **just a few details**; I didn't try to retell *everything* about the text.

_____   In my summary, I explained how all of the events or steps add up to a "big idea."

INSTRUCTIONAL FOCUS: MAIN IDEA AND DETAILS

What's the purpose?

The purpose of this instructional focus is for students to construct basic meaning about informational text. Understanding informational text begins with identifying details and figuring out the main idea. Once these basics have been established, readers can build on this foundation to think about informational text at a deeper level. Some main ideas are stated directly. However, most main ideas need to be inferred. For this reason, some higher-level thinking is necessary for succeeding with this focus—even for basic construction of meaning.

Who would benefit from this focus?

All students need substantial practice in identifying details and determining main ideas. This is especially true for students in the early intermediate grades (grades three and four) and for struggling readers in any grade. But even competent readers need a little extra boost in this area. This focus is challenging because informational text is challenging. Students frequently lack important background knowledge about nonfiction topics; vocabulary is unfamiliar; students may not even be interested in the content and are reading it solely because the chapter has been assigned—for social studies or science or some other academic discipline. The good news is that high-quality informational text is getting easier and easier to find at all reading levels.

What kinds of texts should I use?

The graphics in many informational texts (generally colorful photographs with sharp details) are highly appealing to children, so choose texts that include these alluring visuals. Students should be asked to find the main idea in a portion of a text rather than a whole book, so look for selections with headings. If you can find headings that are presented as questions (*What kind of work would you do if you were a Pilgrim boy?*), that is even better because the simple, one-sentence answer to that question will be the main idea. Another excellent source for identifying main idea and details are alphabet books such as those written by Jerry Pallotta. (Some examples are *The Boat Alphabet Book, The Butterfly Alphabet Book, The Desert Alphabet Book,* and so many more.) In each of these books, the author includes a well-written expository paragraph that describes twenty-six items in each category. For example, in *The Boat Alphabet Book*, there's a description of an aircraft carrier, a barkentine, and a canoe…all the way to *Z is for Zodiac* (an inflatable boat). These short passages are a perfect length for students to locate details and infer the main idea.

What resources will I need for teaching and assessing?

- *Graphic Organizer for Main Idea and Details* (for students to record the details they find and the main idea they infer), page 96
- *Answer Frame for Main Idea and Details: A1-c* (for students to use after they've collected their information on the graphic organizer), page 97
- *Cue Cards for Main Idea and Details* (to be used in the small group to make the task more concrete), page 95
- *Rubric for Finding the Main Idea and Details* (to be used by the teacher to evaluate students' ability to summarize informational text), page 98
- *Checklist for Finding the Main Idea and Details* (to be used by students to reflect on their own skill in summarizing informational text), page 99

How do I implement this?

There's a trick to teaching main idea that I discovered only recently. Most graphic organizers that feature main idea and details show the arrows pointing from the main idea to the details. But this is not the way a kid's mind works. The main idea is an abstraction; the details are concrete. Children are very concrete by nature and, therefore, it is much easier for them to begin their quest for the main idea by first finding the details that the author has stated. Then they should "step back" and decide what all of their details have in common: that's the main idea. In case I'm making this sound *really* easy, know that it is *not*. It's just easier than doing the process in reverse in the usual fashion.

1. Select an informational passage that is at a slightly lower level than a fiction piece you might ask this same group to read. Try to find something that will be interesting to all members of the group (animals usually work well) with few unfamiliar terms.

2. When the group convenes, use the *Target for Summarizing Informational Text* to help students approach the text meaningfully. Begin by discussing the topic and title (or heading), and ask students to predict what they will learn from this part of the text. Look at the structure of the text. How many paragraphs are there? If, for example, there are four paragraphs, point out to students that the author may be giving information about four different ideas. Or perhaps the first paragraph is an introduction in which the author will provide an overview of everything that follows.

3. Remind students to locate the details first and then see what they all have in common in order to figure out the main idea.

4. Place the *Cue Cards for Main Idea and Details* on the reading table. Instruct students to read the first paragraph or the whole text if the selection is short and pick up a "Detail" card when they have located a fact in the text. (Alternately, students can underline the details they find or place a sticky note beneath them.)

5. When everyone in the group has located a detail, discuss the details identified so far and ask if anyone has found enough clues yet to predict what the main idea will be. You can chart the details if this will make them easier for students to review later.

6. Continue reading the text a paragraph at a time following this same instructional pattern until students have finished reading the entire text. Now review all of the details: "Hmm…What do all of these details about the wooly mammoth help us to understand about this animal?" In looking over the details, students conclude that they found out about the many ways that this animal's body helped it to survive the bitter cold of the Ice Age. That's the main idea!

7. Students should complete the *Graphic Organizer for Main Idea and Details* so they can see how their details led them to the main idea of the text.

8. As a follow-up, students can transfer their information to the *Answer Frame for Main Idea and Details* or, if they're really proficient, they can write a brief summary without a frame or organizer. For a written nonfiction summary, all that is needed is a main idea statement and a couple of details to demonstrate a trend.

How do I measure students' success?

Use the criteria identified on the rubric or checklist according to these levels:

Level 1: The student orally identifies the main idea and details.

Level 2: The student identifies the main idea and details on the graphic organizer.

Level 3: The student identifies the main idea and details on the *Answer Frame for Main Idea and Details*.

Level 4: The student identifies the main idea and details independently without using an answer frame or graphic organizer.

Main idea

Detail

Detail

Detail

Detail

Detail

Detail

Detail

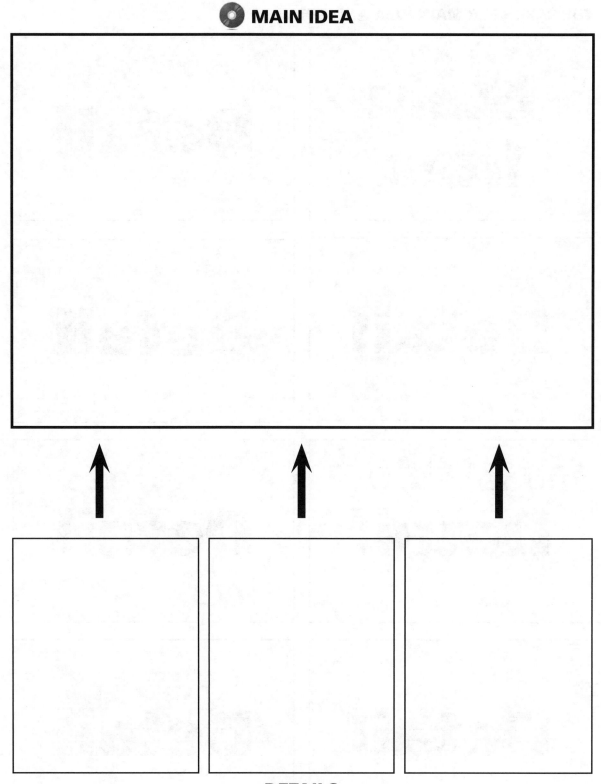

DETAILS

A1-c: What is the main idea of this text/part of the text?

<u>**Strategy for reading**</u>

As you read, look for two or three details in the passage (or a detail from each paragraph if there is more than one paragraph). Think about what all of these details have in common. That will be your main idea! You can write your details on a graphic organizer to help you think about them more clearly.

<u>**Strategy for writing**</u>

1. Tell what the main idea is.
2. Give one detail that shows how you know this is the main idea.
3. Give another detail that shows how you know this is the main idea.

The main idea is _____

_____

_____

_____

One detail that shows this is the main idea is: _____

_____

_____

_____

Another detail that shows this is the main idea is: _____

_____

_____

_____

_____

RUBRIC FOR FINDING THE MAIN IDEA AND DETAILS

NAME: _____ DATE: _____

TEXT: _____

	Excellent (2)	Fair (1)	Poor (0)
Accuracy of main idea	The student correctly identifies the main idea and distinguishes it from the topic	The student identifies a main idea that is close but not exact, or it is more of a "topic"	The student does not accurately identify the main idea
Relevance of details	The student provides details that are relevant to the main idea	The student provides a mix of relevant and irrelevant details	The details are not relevant to the main idea
Elaboration of details	The student provides just enough elaboration to describe the details	The student provides a bit too much or too little elaboration of details	The student includes no elaboration or far too much elaboration
Understanding	The student writes main idea and details in his/her own words demonstrating good comprehension	The student includes a mix of personal wording and wording directly from the text showing some comprehension	The student copies wording directly from the text, showing no real comprehension

Strengths: _____

_____

_____

Areas of need: _____

_____

_____

CHECKLIST FOR SUMMARIZING MAIN IDEA AND DETAILS

NAME: _____ **DATE:** _____

TEXT: _____

❑ I found at least three details about this topic from different parts of this text.

❑ I thought about what all of these details have in common in order to figure out the main idea.

❑ My main idea is a sentence or phrase, not just a "topic" with one or two words.

❑ When I wrote my summary, I started with the main idea and included two details that I described in my own words. (I didn't just copy out of the text.)

The best thing about my informational summary is

_____

_____

_____

To get better at summarizing informational text, I need

_____

_____

_____

Chapter Five

Reinforcing Comprehension Skills and Strategies

TEACHING TO STANDARDS (IS *NOT* TEST PREP!)

Can you handle another principal story? (It's a good one.)

One recent Friday afternoon, a principal friend and I met at a local bistro. It had been a particularly stressful week for both of us, and the prospect of some conversation over a glass of wine sounded appealing. We had barely slid into the booth and placed our order (merlot for my friend, chardonnay for me), when "Merlot" announced "You're not going to believe this."

It seems that one of the administrators from her district's central office had engaged in a conversation not long before this with a group of parents who questioned the elementary schools' recent slide in test scores. This was a sore point for my friend Merlot because, prior to this administration, she had worked diligently to turn around some mediocre scores at her school with more focused instruction aimed at the construction of meaning and explicit attention to state standards. No surprise, the scores headed upward—and stayed there for three happy years. But most recently, under a new administration, there had been another nasty test score dip. A host of different initiatives had emphasized a different instructional model, and the results (those low scores) were not well received by parents and the board of education who wondered *why*.

The district administrator responded: Those earlier scores had been artificially inflated; it was TEST PREP.

First, you have to appreciate the irony here—an administrator making excuses for scores that went *up*! Beyond that, however, there is a more serious discussion that needs to take place: What is the difference between teaching children to read strategically while simultaneously meeting required state and district standards—and overwhelming kids with test-taking strategies so they can just hammer through the test?

Let's be honest here. In order to get good at something, you need to practice it. Providing students with opportunities to practice does not mean you are going over to the Dark Side. Practice is a good thing, but authentic literacy practice must meet several criteria.

CRITERIA FOR AUTHENTIC LITERACY PRACTICE

A valid purpose behind the practice

The standard or objective or whatever defines your purpose must be important to students' literacy development. Truly, this is one of the best features of almost all of the current state standards I've seen and is certainly a hallmark of the Common Core State Standards that we all now share. They do represent the rigor we expect of a worthy literacy curriculum as well as the things we want children to know and be able to do. When I get this "teaching-to-the-test" complaint, the first thing I do is pull out the state or local or Common Core standards and ask the complainer *which ones we should leave out. Summarizing? Making text-to-text connections? Questioning the author?* No, *all* of the standards we typically address really are important for creating strategic readers. Of course, we can miss the mark when we implement the teaching of the standard inappropriately. Or students might be asked to practice something that isn't aligned to any standard. But it's hard to argue against the standards themselves. In fact, the prominence of standards in setting our present educational agenda has done much—at long last—to inspire the mindshift away from teaching that focuses exclusively on literacy *content* to a richer, deeper connection to the purposes for which we read.

A valid task to practice

Writing a response to an open-ended question that measures students' success with a standard is a valid task. It is valid because it is not something students need to do just for "the test." Responding to questions in writing is a mainstay of literature and content-area response throughout students' entire academic career—from about grade two through graduate school. Written response is actually its own genre with characteristics that can be identified, learned, and then practiced. A task that would *not* be so valid in the name of practice would be completing endless multiple-choice questions. When you're reflecting on literature, how often do you give yourself four choices and then rule out the ones that don't work?

A valid place within the instructional sequence

To be instructionally sound, practice needs to assume its rightful place within the gradual release sequence: explain, model, bridge, *practice*, independence. When practice is positioned appropriately, it is authentic. Sometimes teachers ignore the instructional components that need to precede practice, and this renders the practice completely ineffective. Likewise, some teachers get stuck in *practice* mode, never releasing students all the way to independence. This is equally ineffective—and inauthentic. Workbooks and worksheets generate this kind of practice that offers the same level of support day after day after day.

A valid balance among all literacy components

Authentic practice is all about balance. Getting this part wrong is what often gives practice a bad name. So how much practice is enough? Not enough? Too much? Teachers who are convinced that more is better get too wrapped up in written response. *Everything* becomes an opportunity for responding to an open-ended question. I am particularly tired of questions that ask students to make a text-to-self connection. And I'm pretty sure the kids are tired of them, too. When children think that every time they read the tiniest amount of text they will then have to dream up some profound way that this text reminds them of their own life, it's no wonder they produce boring, robotic answers. Students can practice writing answers based on the content of their shared reading text, the text they are reading in their small group, or their independent ("just right") book. But they don't need to respond to all three and definitely not every day. A couple of times per week for a specific standard should do it—for most students. Keep in mind that if practice isn't making perfect, the problem probably lies with the instruction that preceded it. Until you address the underlying cause of the problem, more practice will only reinforce bad habits.

MOVING FORWARD WITH A WHOLE NEW SET OF STANDARDS

The logical place to provide students with practice in meeting literacy standards is during small-group instruction. As described in Chapter Two, this is where we differentiate our teaching with students reading different texts at different levels with different degrees of teacher scaffolding—and for different purposes. In Chapter Four, we explored one purpose that we will need to address regularly with some students: constructing basic meaning. In this chapter, we explore instructional formats for giving students needed practice in meeting literacy standards by reinforcing comprehension skills and strategies. Reality check: all but your most spectacular reading superstars will need to spend considerable small-group time engaged in lessons to reinforce priority standards.

As I've worked in classrooms for the past few years and talked with teachers in districts and in my graduate classes, I addressed the standards I first identified and supported in *That's a GREAT Answer* with strategies for reading and responding, which I later extended with model lessons for shared reading in *Launching RTI Comprehension Instruction*. These were the standards that aligned with most states' grade-level expectations. I expected to show in *this* book how these very same standards could be applied and practiced in a small-group setting to move students to independence.

But wait! There's a whole new set of standards out there now that we need to understand not just within our individual states, but coast to coast—the Common Core State Standards, which address both literacy and math for grades K-12. There are ten comprehension standards at all grade levels grouped into four broad categories: Key Ideas and Details, Craft and Structure, Integration of Knowledge and Ideas, and Range and Level of Text Complexity. There are also sets of standards for Foundational Literacy, Language, Listening and Speaking, and Writing.

Since everyone of us will be accountable to these standards through the curriculum that we design and deliver (in literacy as well as content areas), it would be irresponsible to plan for reinforcing skills and strategies without finding out what's new and adding those new standards to our existing repertoire. And besides, I like the new standards a lot. They have the potential to contribute to literacy teaching and learning in important ways. The ten Common Core State Standards appear below (accessed online at www.corestandards.org).

COLLEGE AND CAREER READINESS STANDARDS FOR READING

Key Ideas and Details

1. Read and closely determine what the text says explicitly and to make logical inferences from it; cite specific textual evidence when writing or speaking to support conclusions drawn from the text.

2. Determine central ideas or themes of a text and analyze their development; summarize the key supporting details and ideas.

3. Analyze in detail where, when, why, and how events, ideas, and characters develop and interact over the course of a text.

Craft and Structure

4. Interpret words and phrases as they are used in a text, including determining technical, connotative, and figurative meanings, and explain how specific word choices shape meaning or tone.

5. Analyze the structure of texts, including how specific sentences, paragraphs, and larger portions of the text relate to each other and the whole.

6. Assess how point of view or purpose shapes the content and style of a text.

Integration of Knowledge and Ideas

7. Synthesize and apply information presented in diverse ways (e.g., through words, images, graphs, and video) in print and digital sources in order to answer questions, solve problems, or compare modes of presentation.

8. Delineate and evaluate the reasoning and rhetoric within a text, including assessing whether the evidence provided is relevant and sufficient to support the text's claims. (nonfiction)

9. Analyze how two or more texts address similar themes or topics in order to build knowledge or to compare the approaches the authors take.

Range and Level of Text Complexity

10. Read complex texts independently, proficiently, and fluently, sustaining concentration, monitoring comprehension, and when useful, rereading.

You will need to decide for yourself how closely your state standards align with the CCSS. You might especially want to view your state's standards in terms of major trends that seem to be present within the Common Core State Standards. The trends, as I perceive them, are noted in the next section.

TRENDS IN THE COMMON CORE STATE STANDARDS

Key features of the Common Core State Standards include:

- A systematic and incremental progression of rigor within each standard from grade to grade (staircase standards)

- Lots of focus on critical thinking within all 10 standards

- Lots of focus on vocabulary (particularly word choice as an element of author's craft)

- Lots of focus on discussion (identified within the Listening and Speaking standards)

- Lots of focus on new (digital) literacies

- Lots of focus on visual literacy (recognizing that graphics and illustrations contribute to the author's message)

- Lots of focus on author's craft

- Lots of focus on text structure and genre as aids to comprehension

- Lots of focus on synthesis of two or more texts

- Lots of focus on author's voice (point of view, bias) in creating meaning

- An entire standard (10) devoted to fluency at grade level, independent reading, and use of comprehension strategies as a means of enhancing comprehension

- No focus on text-to-self connections/reactions (C1, C2)

- Little emphasis on creative thinking (extending the text: D2)

IDENTIFYING A NEW AND IMPROVED LIST OF STANDARDS AND OBJECTIVES

When you analyze the objectives I identified in *That's a Great Answer* and *Launching RTI Comprehension Instruction*, it is clear that most of those objectives hit the mark perfectly. I would not remove anything. Although the Common Core State Standards do not allow "cherry picking"—selecting which standards you want, and those you don't—states can add up to fifteen percent to the CCSS from standards they value in their own state that didn't make it onto the common list. Given the opportunity, I would choose to add back C1 and C2 (text-to-self connections) and D2 (extending the text—which taps students' creative thinking). I would also add three new standards based on the increased rigor of the Common Core: Determine meaning from context (A5); make connections between texts (C3); and integrate and evaluate content presented in diverse media and formats (D4).

Thirteen new objectives would be added to the new and improved array for a total of 53 specific objectives. While these specific objectives capture the intent of each standard, teachers will need to look closely at the Common Core State Standards document itself to determine exactly what is expected of students *at each grade level*. My revised list of standards and objectives is as follows. New standards are boxed and shaded. Note also that next to each standard in bold print is the comprehension strategy with which it is aligned. The type of text that could be used to meet the standard—fiction or nonfiction—is indicated in parentheses.

COMPREHENSION STANDARDS AND OBJECTIVES

The "A" Strand: Forming a General Understanding
A1: Main idea and theme
- **A1-a**: What lesson does _____ learn in this story? (fiction) **[figuring out]**
- **A1-b**: What is the theme of this story? (fiction) **[figuring out]**
- **A1-c**: What is the main idea? (nonfiction) **[figuring out]**
- **A1-d**: What would be another good title for this book/story? (fiction, nonfiction) **[figuring out]**

A2: Characters, problem/solution, setting
- **A2-a**: Using information in the story, write a brief description of how _____ felt when…. (fiction) **[figuring out]**
- **A2-b**: What is _____'s main problem in the story? Give details from the story to support your answer. (fiction) **[noticing]**
- **A2-c**: How did _____ solve his/her problem? Give details from the story to support your answer. (fiction) **[noticing]**
- **A2-d**: How did _____ change from the beginning to the end of the story? (fiction) **[figuring out]**
- **A2-e**: What is the setting of this story? Give details from the story to support your answer. (fiction) **[noticing]**

- **A2-f:** Describe this character based on his/her thoughts, words, deeds, or interactions with others. (fiction) **[figuring out]**

A3: Summarizing
- **A3-a:** Briefly summarize this story **incorporating theme**. (fiction) **[figuring out]**
- **A3-b:** Summarize the main things that happened in this [book]. (fiction, nonfiction) **[figuring out]**
- **A3-c:** Briefly summarize this article/informational text. (nonfiction) **[figuring out]**

- **A3-d:** <u>Paraphrase</u> a story, fable, folktale, or myth (including texts from diverse cultures), incorporating the lesson, moral, or theme **(grade 2)**. (fiction) **[figuring out]**

A4: Predicting
- **A4-a:** Predict what will happen next in this story. (fiction) [guessing/predicting]
- **A4-b:** If the author added another paragraph to the end of the story (or article), it would <u>most likely</u> tell about _____. Use information from the story (or article) to support your answer. (fiction, nonfiction) [guessing/predicting]

A5: Determine meaning from context

- **A5-a:** Determine the meaning of words and phrases as they are used in a text, including figurative language. (fiction/nonfiction) **[figuring out]**
- **A5-b:** Determine the meaning of general academic and domain-specific words or phrases in a text relevant to a grade-level topic or subject area. (fiction/nonfiction) **[figuring out]**

The "B" Strand: Developing an Interpretation

B1: Identify or infer the author's use of structure/organizational patterns
- **B1-a:** What caused _____ to happen in the story? (fiction) **[noticing]**
- **B1-b:** What happened at the beginning, in the middle, and at the end of the story? (fiction) **[noticing]**
- **B1-c:** Compare these two characters. (fiction) **[noticing]**
- **B1-d:** Can this part of the [story/text] be described as: a description, an explanation, a conversation, an opinion, an argument, or a comparison? How do you know? (fiction, nonfiction) **[noticing]**

- **B1-e:** What is the genre of this text and what are the characteristics of this genre? (fiction) **[noticing]**

B2: Draw conclusions about the author's purpose for choosing a genre or for including or omitting specific details in text
- **B2-a:** Why does the author include paragraph ___? (fiction, nonfiction) **[figuring out]**
- **B2-b:** Why did the author write a [poem/story/nonfiction book] about this? (fiction, nonfiction) **[figuring out]**

B3: Use evidence from the text to support a conclusion
- **B3-a:** Prove that [character/person] is very _____. (fiction, nonfiction) **[figuring out]**
- **B3-b:** Which facts show that _____? (fiction, nonfiction) **[noticing]**

- **B3-c:** Trace and evaluate the argument and specific claims in a text, assessing whether the reasoning is sound and the evidence is relevant and sufficient to support the claims. (nonfiction) **(grade 7 and above) [noticing]**

The "C" Strand: Making reader/text connections
C1: Connect the text to a personal experience, another text, or the outside world
- **C1-a:** Make a personal connection to the *experience* in the story. (fiction) **[connecting]**
- **C1-b:** Make a personal connection to a *feeling* in the story. (fiction) **[connecting]**
- **C1-c:** Would you like _____ for a friend? Why or why not? (fiction, nonfiction) **[connecting]**
- **C1-d:** Using information in the story, explain whether you would ever want to _____. (fiction, nonfiction) **[connecting]**

C2: Make a personal response to the text
- **C2-a:** Which part of the story/article do you think was *most* important? Use information from the story to explain why you chose that part. (fiction, nonfiction) **[connecting]**
- **C2-b:** Which part of this [story/article] was most interesting or surprising to you? Why? (fiction, nonfiction) **[connecting]**
- **C2-c:** Did you like this [story/article]? Why or why not? (fiction, nonfiction) **[connecting]**
- **C2-d:** What was your first reaction to this text? Explain. (fiction, nonfiction) **[connecting]**

C-3: Make connections between texts

- **C3-a:** Compare/contrast two or more versions of the same story. (fiction) **[connecting]**
- **C3-b:** Compare/contrast the treatment of similar themes and topics in different texts. (fiction) **[connecting]**
- **C3-c:** Integrate information from two or more texts on the same topic in order to write or speak about the topic. (nonfiction) **[connecting]**

The "D" Strand: Examining content and structure
D1: Examine the author's craft
- **D1-a:** Choose [2] words from paragraph ___ that help you picture the _____. (fiction, nonfiction) **[picturing]**
- **D1-b:** Choose a simile and explain why the author chose that simile. (fiction, nonfiction) **[noticing]**
- **D1-c:** How did the author create humor in paragraph _____? (fiction) **[noticing]**
- **D1-d:** Give an example of personification in paragraph ____. (fiction) **[noticing]**
- **D1-e:** Do you think the author made this story believable? Why or why not? (fiction) **[figuring out]**

- **D1-f:** Explain the effect of literary devices (author's crafts) such as flashbacks and foreshadowing on the development of plot and meaning. (fiction) **(grade 6 and above) [figuring out]**
- **D1-g:** From whose point of view is this story told (or information provided)? How does that influence meaning? (fiction) **[figuring out]**

D2: Extend the text

- **D2-a:** What two questions would you like to ask the author that were not answered in this text? (fiction, nonfiction) **[wondering]**
- **D2-b:** Imagine you are going to give a talk to your class about _____. What two points would you be sure to include in your speech? (nonfiction) **[figuring out]**
- **D2-c:** Using information in the text, write a paragraph that could have appeared in ____'s journal after _____ occurred. (fiction, nonfiction) **[figuring out]**

D3: Show that you understand what was important to an author or character

- **D3-a:** How does the author/character show that _____ is important to him/her? (fiction, nonfiction) **[noticing]**
- **D3-b:** How are your customs different from the customs described in this story/ article? (fiction, nonfiction) **[figuring out]**

D4: Integrate and evaluate content presented in diverse media and formats

- **D4-a:** Explain how specific aspects of a text's illustrations contribute to what is conveyed by the words in a story or in an informational text. (fiction/nonfiction) **[visualizing]**
- **D4-b:** Compare and contrast the experience of reading a literary or an informational text to listening to or viewing an audio, video, or live version of that text. (fiction/nonfiction) **[figuring out]**

Missing from this list are the components of a comprehensive literacy curriculum embedded in standard ten of the Common Core standards: *Read complex texts independently, proficiently, and fluently, sustaining concentration, monitoring comprehension, and when useful, rereading.* Note the inherent concepts here: independence, fluency, and monitoring comprehension. These concepts ask us to strengthen students' capacity for:

- Independent reading with stamina,
- Fluency at grade level, and
- Use of comprehension strategies to monitor thinking.

While these are not the kinds of objectives teachers can teach to "mastery," they are goals that we need to wrap into our literacy curriculum, too—on a daily basis. With all of this in mind, we need to craft focused small-group lessons that address specific comprehension objectives and strategies aimed at the attainment of literacy standards.

This chapter then provides protocols for the explicit small-group teaching of specific comprehension objectives and for specific applications of individual comprehension strategies (for teachers who wish to pursue standards via the metacognitive strategies). It also offers guidelines for lessons enhancing comprehension of a selected text through focused lessons in fluency, vocabulary, and author's craft.

Before embarking on an explanation of each of these instructional formats, however, I want to propose a general order for addressing objectives, so we treat the *cause* of students' comprehension needs, not just the *symptoms*. See the chart on page 111 titled *Building Understanding from the Ground up*. Although this is a concept I have discussed with teachers for a few years now, I have recently revised this chart slightly to align more consistently with the Common Core State Standards.

The objectives you see at the base are those that students must grasp before moving on to the "Keep Climbing" level , for the objectives in this second band build on those at the base. Likewise, students should "climb" through that second level to "Reach the Summit," which requires competence with *all* preceding objectives in order to succeed.

The reason this chart is so crucial to small-group instruction is that teachers' first thought when students are having difficulty with a concept is often "This kid needs more practice with…" But the reality is that students may be having a problem with, for example, summarizing because they have not quite gotten the hang of a prerequisite skill: identifying theme or recognizing story elements. No amount of additional practice is going to "fix" the summarizing situation unless you first address those story parts and the big idea of the story. This does not mean that you need to spend months and months teaching theme and story parts before you can expect students to create a summary. It does mean that you may need a series of lessons around a particular text—perhaps determining story elements on the first day, working on theme a second day, and then finally getting to the task of summarizing. When students have a more independent command of theme and story parts, you will be able to get to that summary more expediently.

The particular objectives or strategies you choose to reinforce in your small-group instruction should directly correlate with your assessment data. The data can be as formal as the results from your last state assessment and periodic RTI progress-monitoring instruments. Or it can be as informal as your observations of students' performance the last time you met with them in their small group. The instructional protocols that follow in this chapter for comprehension objectives and comprehension strategy applications, as well as lesson formats for fluency, vocabulary instruction, and author's craft, will give you plenty of options for reinforcing students' specific skill and strategy needs.

BUILDING UNDERSTANDING FROM THE GROUND UP

REACH THE SUMMIT

- B2: Author's reason for including/omitting information
- D2: Extending the text
- D3: Author's/character's customs/values
- C3: Text-to-text connections
- D4: Integrating content in diverse media

KEEP CLIMBING

- A3: Summarizing
- B1: Text structure/genre
- C1: Personal connections
- C2: Personal reaction
- D1: Author's craft

BEGIN AT THE BASE

- A2: Story elements, sequence of events, important facts
- A1: Theme, main idea
- A4: Making predictions
- B3: Finding evidence to support a conclusion
- A5: Determining word meaning from context

Consider the following reflection questions before turning to the instructional formats for reinforcing skills and strategies. This will make your reading of the remainder of this chapter more purposeful.

QUESTIONS TO CONSIDER

1. What do you do to ensure that your students meet grade-level standards?

2. Do you address standards through whole-class (shared) instruction? Small-group instruction? Both? How?

3. Give an example of something you ask your students to do that you consider *authentic* practice.

4. Give an example of something that you do *not* consider to be authentic practice.

5. What is the next step when your students do not meet grade-level standards?

6. What questions do you hope the remainder of this chapter will answer for you?

INSTRUCTIONAL FOCUS: SPECIFIC COMPREHENSION OBJECTIVES (STRANDS A-D)

What's the purpose?

The purpose of this instructional focus is to reinforce specific comprehension objectives introduced during shared reading by providing students with text at their instructional level that they will read. This developmentally appropriate text allows students to practice meeting the objective under the close guidance of their classroom teacher. The ultimate goal is for students to achieve independence with the objective, typically measured through students' written responses to open-ended comprehension questions.

The emphasis in this kind of lesson should be on helping students read *strategically* to find the evidence to meet a particular objective. This means we will explain *up front* (in the "Before Reading" portion of the lesson) how to monitor thinking *during* reading in order to know at the end of the chapter or the poem or whatever the specific evidence needed to make a personal connection, determine the structure of a text, or identify a character trait. Focused, standards-based teaching of this sort goes well beyond *having* a focus (a critical first step) to *being* strategic. If we are serious about helping readers achieve grade-level standards at the RTI Tier 1 level, we need to embrace this notion of strategic reading—even when we are not teaching comprehension strategies as we have come to know them: connecting, picturing, predicting, etc.

The target template (page 117) included as a resource in this chapter serves as a reminder not just that we need a clearly defined objective if we intend for students to meet specific literacy standards, but that the language of that objective must be kid-friendly, targeted to students' to capacity to understand. Moreover, the target itself is followed by a few easy-to-follow steps—a road map to meeting the objective.

Other components of a high-quality focused comprehension lesson are indicated in the *Instructional Map for an Explicit Standards-based RTI Tier 1 Comprehension Lesson* (page 116). I don't like to ask teachers to fill out a lesson plan with all of these components written down; if you're planning for multiple groups every day, this is a lot of writing and would probably not do much to encourage you to incorporate small-group instruction into your literacy curriculum on a regular basis. So, just fill out the much less labor-intensive *Small-group Planner* on page 43 in the Introduction to Part II of this book and refer to the *Instructional Map* on page 116 to maximize the power of your explicit lesson.

Who would benefit from this focus?

This instructional focus is especially useful for students who are not making sufficient progress with an objective through classroom shared-reading lessons alone. (This will likely be most students in your class—at least *some* of the time.) The intent is to provide additional practice on the shared reading objective with text at students' instructional level or to address prerequisite objectives that students may need to master before they can successfully navigate the grade-level standard. This differentiated support is an essential component of RTI Tier 1 instruction for *all* students and can often eliminate the need for Tier 2 interventions for readers who might struggle if literacy instruction remained solely at the whole-class level. Small-group instruction focused on specific comprehension objectives can also be useful to students working on or above grade level by applying the objective to more challenging texts or by requiring students to meet more rigorous standards that encourage thinking typically reserved for a higher grade level.

What kinds of texts should I use?

Because the instruction leading to mastery of a specific comprehension objective is necessarily very focused, short text with multiple opportunities to apply the objective is especially helpful. (See the bibliography of short texts on in the Introduction to Part II on pages 44-48 for suggestions for your grade level.) Additionally, as many state assessments incorporate a large proportion of informational text, teachers should make a special effort to select short informational pieces when teaching lessons aligned with these objectives.

What resources will I need for teaching and assessing?

- *Comprehension Standards and Objectives* (a list of objectives suitable for a small-group or shared lesson focus), pages 106-109

- *Instructional Map for an Explicit Standards-based RTI Tier 1 Comprehension Lesson* (a useful document for teachers to keep handy during small-group and shared reading instruction to keep their focused comprehension lesson on track), page 116

- **Target sheets matched to each objective that explain how to find the best evidence to meet the objective** (matched to the forty generic targets identified in my book, *Launching RTI Comprehension Instruction with Shared Reading: 40 Lessons for Intermediate Readers*), CD folder: "Target Sheets"

- **Target template** (a target—and how to reach the target—is useful for all focus areas but is essential for teaching specific comprehension objectives; teachers can determine their own targets along with criteria for finding evidence for objectives not included on the list of forty objectives on pages 106-109), page 117

- **Answer organizers and answer frames** (see templates in two of my previous books, *That's a GREAT Answer* and *Teaching Written Response to Text*, which contain graphic organizers for both long and short constructed responses)

- *Rubric for Assessing Students' Oral and Written Response to Text* (for teachers to assess students), page 118

- *Written-Response Check Sheet* (for students' self-reflection on oral and written response), page 119

How do I implement this?

1. Examine student assessment data, including anecdotal observations during shared-reading lessons and previous small-group lessons that address specific objectives. Who doesn't "get it?" Is the identified poor performance solely a function of *this* objective? Or is poor performance on this objective more of a symptom of a problem caused by failure to meet some prerequisite standard?

2. For this focus area above all others, teachers need to know *why* they are choosing a particular objective to teach during small-group instruction; be sure you can identify *WHY* using reliable data. (You should *always* be able to answer this question.)

3. Lessons focused on specific comprehension objectives begin with the teacher **explaining** the objective that references the target (how to find evidence to meet the objective).

4. **Model** the application of the objective with a couple of examples from the first chunk of text. If you are working on a particular objective over several days, each succeeding day should require less modeling until *no* modeling is necessary.

5. Ask students to read (silently) the next short chunk of text in order to **practice** finding evidence to meet the objective; students can validate their evidence by reading aloud the relevant portions of text.*

6. Continue reading in this fashion with students finding and sharing multiple pieces of evidence that meet the objective.*

7. When students have finished the reading, provide an **oral rehearsal** of the response aligned with the objective.

8. As a follow-up activity, students may complete a **written response** to the same question (aligned with the objective) if appropriate. Note, though, that all lessons do *not* need to culminate in a written response.

*When students have become more proficient with a particular objective, expect them to do more of the reading independently. Instead of doing all of the reading right in the group, send them back to their seats to finish. They can mark the evidence in their text with sticky notes and be prepared to discuss it the next time their group meets.

How do I measure students' success?

Accurate, organized, and suitably elaborated responses that meet the state-identified criteria:

Level 1: Oral response that meets the criteria for the objective—including complete sentences with appropriate vocabulary

Level 2: Written response that is scaffolded with an aligned answer organizer or answer frame

Level 3: Written response that is completed independently without the aid of graphic support.

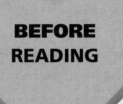

INSTRUCTIONAL MAP FOR AN EXPLICIT STANDARDS-BASED
RTI TIER 1 COMPREHENSION LESSON

BEFORE READING

- Activate prior knowledge
- Make predictions
- Set purpose (clarify the objective/target)
- Introduce vocabulary as appropriate
- Explain *how* to find evidence for the objective (make the reading strategic)

DURING READING

- Model how you find the evidence
- Provide time for students to practice finding evidence—prompted or unprompted
- Apply other strategies as appropriate (without losing the focus of the lesson)
- Address vocabulary as needed

AFTER READING

- Orally rehearse the response matched to the lesson objective
- Write a response to a question matched to the lesson objective

_____

_____

_____

How to hit the target:

RUBRIC FOR ASSESSING STUDENTS' ORAL AND WRITTEN RESPONSE TO COMPREHENSION QUESTIONS

NAME: _____ DATE: _____

QUESTION: _____

	2 = Excellent	**1 = Developing**	**0 = Below Basic**
Accuracy	The answer is completely accurate. It is clearly based on events in the text that really happened, correctly represents factual information, and formulates reasonable inferences.	The answer is partially accurate. It shows some confusion about events or information described in the text, and inferences may be far fetched or not tied directly to the content of the reading.	The answer is inaccurate and is well below the range of grade-level expectations. It is not clear that the student has constructed basic meaning from the text, either explicit or inferred.
Organization	The answer is logically organized. It follows the steps specified in the response criteria or uses another sequential structure that makes sense to the reader.	The answer is marginally organized. It may begin in a logical fashion but loses its focus, or the parts may all be present but are not well sequenced.	The answer has no organizational framework and is well below the range of grade-level expectations. It may be too sparse to provide a sense of organization; it may be very long and repetitive, saying the same thing over and over in a variety of ways; or it may be largely incoherent with no sense of direction.
Thoroughness	The answer is thorough according to grade-level expectations. It meets all criteria for details and elaboration specified for the response to a particular question. The details show a close, careful reading of the text.	The answer is more general than specific. It contains some details and elaboration, but the student has missed or has neglected to include enough evidence from the text to sufficiently support a general statement or main idea.	The answer is vague and/or irrelevant and is well below the range of grade-level expectations. It may be so general, far fetched, or loosely tied to the text that it is hard to tell whether the student has even read the text.
Fluency	The answer flows smoothly. It demonstrates grade-level-appropriate competence with grammar, usage, writing conventions, vocabulary, and language structure.	The answer sounds somewhat "choppy." It is generally able to be read and understood but may show more carelessness or lack of proficiency in the use of grammar, usage, writing conventions, vocabulary, and language structure than is appropriate for a student at this grade level.	The answer is nearly incomprehensible because of written language deficits and is well below the range of grade-level expectations. It shows extreme lack of skill in communicating ideas in writing and may signal the need for interventions beyond the scope of written-response instructional supports.

Greatest strength: _____

_____

Next steps: _____

_____

NAME: _____ DATE: _____

QUESTION: _____

I think my score on this question would be _____ .

❏   My answer is <u>correct</u>. The information came right from what I read.

❏   My answer is <u>organized</u>. It makes sense when I read it. It has a good order.

❏   My answer has plenty of <u>details</u>. It has examples or other evidence from the text.

❏   My answer is <u>written</u> so people can read it easily. I didn't leave words out. I tried to spell carefully. I remembered capitals and periods.

The best thing about my answer is _____

_____

_____ .

I still need to work on _____

_____

_____ .

INSTRUCTIONAL FOCUS:
FOCUSED COMPREHENSION STRATEGY APPLICATIONS

What's the purpose?

Sometimes teachers want to approach students' literacy development entirely through comprehension strategies rather than through the kind of standards-based objectives described in the previous portion of this chapter. I regard this as something of a luxury in today's data-driven world, where what we teach is often directly correlated to what we need to measure. It is certainly possible to feature comprehension strategies at all points within the instructional cycle: constructing basic meaning, reinforcing specific reading competencies, and finally, engaging in higher-level thinking about text through discussion. In Chapter Four, I offered two formats for using comprehension strategies to construct initial understanding—one at a basic level and the other, more advanced. Here I carry forward the application of comprehension strategies with suggestions for lessons that reinforce particular aspects of each strategy.

Who would benefit from this focus?

When you introduce comprehension strategies as a repertoire as I suggest in Chapter Four (and also in my book, *Constructing Meaning through Kid-Friendly Comprehension Strategy Instruction*), you will notice two things. First, kids are pretty good at using the strategies—right away. Because these are techniques that readers use quite naturally (albeit subconsciously) to understand what they read, students navigate their way through the process fairly successfully, completing their reading with adequate knowledge of fundamental text elements. You will also notice, however, that students' strategy use is a bit rough around the edges based on their initial attempts. They would surely benefit from opportunities to refine their strategic thinking. Hence I would say that this lesson format would be most helpful to students who have been introduced to the strategies earlier on for basic construction of meaning and now want to hone strategies for deeper thinking.

What kinds of texts should I use?

Almost any kind of text will work for this instructional focus. However, because the intent here is to refine applications of individual strategies, you need to select texts where using that one main strategy would truly enhance comprehension. The following suggestions are not the *only* types of texts that would be appropriate, but these will at least give you a place to begin.

For noticing
- Texts with a clear structure (story elements, sequence, main idea/details, etc.)
- Texts with a variety of author's crafts represented
- Texts with well-developed characters (where the author has defined characters with dialogue, actions, appearance, etc.)
- Informational text with lots of text features (captions, bold print, diagrams, etc.)
- Picture books where the illustrations contribute to the message in significant ways

For making text-to-self connections
- Realistic fiction where the characters are approximately the same age as your students and face similar problems with family, friends, school, etc.
- Any text with a theme to which students can readily relate

For text-to-text connections
- Two or more texts with similar themes or problems
- Two or more texts about the same person or people with similar life experiences

For wondering
- Texts that explore moral or ethical dilemmas, such as the Holocaust, slavery, civil rights, and immigration
- Informational texts that make readers curious to learn more about the topic

For predicting
- Problem/solution texts with plenty of action
- Texts that "leave you hanging" at the end, anticipating a possible next page or chapter

For picturing
- Poetry or other text that includes lots of imagery and description
- Personal narratives that evoke a reader's own memories

For figuring out (inferring)
- Texts with a strong message or theme such as fables, myths, and legends
- Texts with well-developed characters whose traits become evident through their thoughts, words, deeds, and interactions with others
- Texts where there is lots of "showing" and little "telling"

For figuring out (synthesizing/summarizing)
- Narrative: Texts that contain clear story elements, such as fairytales and most other problem/solution texts
- Informational: Texts with fairly obvious main ideas and lots of supporting details

What resources will I need for teaching and assessing?

- *Strategy Points for Focus Lessons* (teaching points for lessons to apply comprehension strategies more deeply), pages 123-128
- *Instructional Map for an Explicit Comprehension Strategy Lesson* (a useful document for teachers to keep handy during small-group and shared reading instruction to keep their explicit strategy lesson on track), page 129
- *Strategy Follow-up Activities* (follow-up tasks on individual strategies found in *Constructing Meaning* will be especially helpful for reinforcing students' use of specific strategies), pages 153-197
- *Rubric for Using Individual Strategies Accurately and Insightfully* (for the teacher to assess students), page 130
- *Checklist for Using Individual Comprehension Strategies* (for student self-reflections), page 131

How do I implement this?

1. As you observe students constructing basic meaning using the repertoire of comprehension strategies, you will see which strategies they navigate well, and which ones need more attention. Select a specific strategy focus based on students' demonstrated needs: Are they having difficulty identifying how an author builds suspense? Making predictions based on genre? Creating pictures in their mind with multiple senses? (Note that you are working with one particular application of a strategy, not an entire strategy—*predicting, picturing,* etc.)

2. Teach this lesson as you would any explicit lesson. (See the *Instructional Map for an Explicit Comprehension Strategy Lesson* on page 129 for a more detailed lesson sequence.) Begin with an **explanation** of how to apply the strategy. This might include tips for where to apply the strategy within the text or something you do in your own reading to use a strategy effectively.

3. If this strategy application is new or fairly new to students, you will want to **model** it in a couple of key places.

4. Then students need to **practice**. This might occur right in the group with the teacher present for guidance. In this case, students will most likely read short chunks of text, reflecting on their strategy use after each one. Or, if the group is capable of more independence, students may be sent back to their seats to continue to apply the strategy themselves—along with clear directions for what they are expected to accomplish: "Mark two places with sticky notes where you used this strategy." "Jot a sentence in your reader's notebook about how this strategy helped you today." There are lots of simple ways to encourage students to monitor their strategy use.

5. An explicit strategy lesson should always conclude with **reflection** on the use of the strategy. There should always be oral reflection: "How did this strategy help you as a reader? What was easy? What was difficult? How can I help you learn to use this strategy even more effectively?" If you wish to obtain some written documentation of students' ability to use a particular strategy, consider using one of the *Strategy Follow-up Activities* in my book, *Constructing Meaning through Kid-Friendly Comprehension Strategy Instruction*. There are about fifty tasks in that book that address individual strategy use for both literary and informational text.

How do I measure students' success?

1. **Level 1:** Uses the target strategy accurately, though insights are limited and the student may continue to need significant teacher guidance

2. **Level 2:** Uses the strategy accurately and insightfully with some teacher guidance at times

3. **Level 3:** Uses the target strategy accurately and insightfully without teacher support

STRATEGY POINTS FOR FOCUS LESSONS

Each bulleted point can be the focus of a small-group lesson aimed at enhancing students' use of individual metacognitive comprehension strategies. In each case, strategic thinking is supported by helping readers recognize *how* to apply the strategy and *where* the strategy will most likely be applied in the text. You might be able to include more than one point in a lesson.

NOTICING		
How **to be a good "noticer"**	*What* **to notice in a story**	*What* **to notice in informational text**
• Pause as you read • Have an "inner conversation" about what you are reading (or think aloud if that works better for you) • Underline parts of the text that seem important to you • Use sticky notes to remind you about something you think is important • Write notes in the margin • Be selective—don't underline *everything* • Jot down thoughts and reactions in a reading journal • Go back to reread to fix up meaning • Use one or more comprehension strategies to keep your mind engaged • Stay focused on your reading; if you get distracted, you'll miss lots of important clues	• Characters' names • What a character cares about • Special features about the setting where the story takes place • Something odd that you didn't expect to happen • The turning point • Great words that you might want to use in your writing • The way the author gets you hooked on the story • The way the author builds suspense • What the author did to make the ending memorable • The way the illustrations make the story even more powerful • The way the author organized the story (is it problem/solution or *first, next, then...*)? • When something doesn't make sense • Places where the author is hoping you'll picture or wonder or use another thinking strategy	• Names of people—especially if something is written about them • Dates—especially if something is written about them • Bulleted lists • Words in italics or bold font or bigger font • The number of paragraphs about one topic (more paragraphs probably means this is important) • Graphics (they let you know what is important on that page) • Captions—you can get a lot of good information without reading a whole lot • The first paragraph of every article, the last paragraph of every article, and the first sentence of each paragraph • The questions at the end of the chapter—these let you know important points you should look for as you read • Words that you don't understand • Don't try to find one "most important part." In informational text, many ideas have the same importance

PICTURING	
How to make good pictures in your mind	**_Where_ to find a good mental picture**
• Pretend you're making a movie: What would you put in this scene? • Pretend you're drawing a picture: What details would you include in your picture? • Try to picture: the expression on someone's face; the body language; the tone of voice • Identify a snapshot in the text • Describe the image in the author's words • Use all of your senses to "see" the picture • Extend the picture: What else could be in the picture that the author doesn't mention? • Recognize words and other author's crafts that help you see the picture in your mind • Try to picture the story from a different point of view (Ex: How would a different character in the story see this situation?)	• Passages with lots of describing words or action words • Passages where someone is talking or people are having a conversation • Passages where people are expressing some kind of emotion—like yelling at each other, crying, or showing happiness or excitement • Passages that make you laugh—or cry • Passages that remind you of something that happened to you • Passages that are about something gross or scary • Passages where you can predict a problem is going to occur because of something that someone did • Passages that are so important that they stick in your brain even when you don't want them there

WONDERING	
How to ask a good question about a book	**Where** to find a good question
• Remember the question words (*who, what, when, where, why, how*). • Think: *Is this a question that will really help me to understand this [story] better?* • Is this a question that needs more than a one-word answer (like *yes* or *no*)? • Consider: *What kinds of things do you think the author wants me to wonder about?* • Good readers often wonder why characters behave in certain ways; this leads to better understanding of the story. • If you think of a question that you could answer on your own without reading the [story], it probably isn't a good question to be asking. • Questions that make you think are usually more important than questions with answers that are right in the book.	• Books about something unfair or something that is troubling in some way will probably lead to lots of really important questions. • Nonfiction books about topics you know *something* about, but not *a lot* about, will lead to questions about other things you'd like to know. • "Silly" books usually don't lead to great questions. • The title of the book, the picture on the cover, or the blurb on the back may lead to some good questions *before* you read. • Wondering about what will happen next often leads to good questions (and predictions) *during* reading. • Sometimes a story ends before it feels "finished." This is a good place to wonder what would probably happen next. • At the end of a book about a topic that is very troubling, good readers often wonder what makes people/characters behave so badly.

PREDICTING (GUESSING)		
How to get good at predicting	*Where* to make a prediction when you read a story	*Where* to make a prediction when you read informational text
• Most important: When you read a *story*, you predict what will *happen*. When you read a *nonfiction text*, you predict what you will *learn*. • Make sure that your prediction makes sense: Did something that already happened lead to your prediction about what will probably happen next? (Your prediction shouldn't just be what you *want* to happen.) • Sometimes the title helps you to predict what will happen in a story, but sometimes the title is more confusing than helpful. Don't spend too much time making predictions based on a title. • It is always good to notice who the author is because if you know the author, you can usually make some good predictions about what the book will be like. • If you know what kind of text you're reading, you'll be able to predict something about it. For example, if you know the story is a *fable*, you will try to predict the *lesson*. • Think about where the author wants you to predict. For example, is there a "cliff hanger" at the end of a chapter? Does the author build suspense before the mystery gets solved? • Don't get bogged down in predictions. Predictions do help you to stay focused on your reading because you are curious to find out if what you predict actually happens. But using your other strategies will help you to stay focused, too—and sometimes other strategies can lead to even deeper understanding.	• Before you read the story when you check the title, the author's name, and the blurb on the back • Before you read when you think about what the genre is • During reading when you think about what will probably happen next • After reading when you think about what could happen if the author added another paragraph or chapter.	• Look at the title. That will give you a *general* idea what you will learn. • Look at the table of contents (especially the titles of the chapters). That will give you *specific* ideas about what you will learn. • Look at the bolded subheadings in a chapter and try to turn each subheading into a question. That will help you predict what you will learn about in that part of the text. • Look at the graphics (maps, photographs, diagrams, etc.). These will also let you predict what you will learn about.

FIGURING OUT		
***How* to figure out**	***Where* and *when* to synthesize (summarize)**	***Where* and *when* to infer**
• In both stories and informational text, there are things the author wants you to understand, even though he or she doesn't tell you directly; you have to look for clues as you read and figure out the meaning on your own. • There are different ways to "figure out" the meaning of a text. • You can add up all the clues and figure out how all the pieces fit together. That is *synthesizing* (which we can think of as *summarizing*). • Or, you can figure out the "big idea"—the message the author wants you to get as you read the words. That is *inferring*.	• As you're reading a story—keep summarizing it in your mind to make sure you are understanding it so far. (This is especially important when you've read part of the story the day before and come back the next day to finish it.) • When you've finished the story—summarize to make sure that you know all of the story parts (characters, setting, problem, etc.) or that you know the events in sequence when it is not a problem/solution text. • When you are reading nonfiction—summarize to figure out the main idea (summarize the details and see what they all have in common). • When you have read more than one text about a topic and want to combine all of the information you've learned into one "file in your brain"—summarize with information from both sources.	• While you are reading—infer when you want to make a prediction about what might happen next. • While you are reading—infer when you want to figure out how the problem will get solved. • While you are reading—infer when you are trying to understand a character better (like feelings or their character traits). • While you are reading—infer as you try to figure out why the author included a particular line or paragraph. • While you are reading—infer as you figure out the "big idea" or theme (you can infer about the big idea and theme after reading, too). • After reading—infer when you want to figure out the author's purpose for writing the text.

CONNECTING AND REACTING

How to make good connections or share thoughtful reactions	*What* kinds of connections to look for	*What* kinds of reactions to look for
• Don't try to connect right at the beginning of the text. • Figure out the "big idea" as you read before making a connection. • Make a connection to the "big idea." • Do not make a connection just to your background knowledge; that is a <u>coincidence</u>. • Choose your own detail that matches the big idea—not the same detail the author chose. • Your reaction will come from your *heart* more than your *mind*; think about your *feelings*.	• Experience: What is the "big" experience that the author wants you to think about? Has something like this ever happened to you? • Feeling: What is the feeling that the author wants you to understand? When have you felt this way? • Theme: What lesson can people in general learn from the experience of this book? When has this lesson been important in *your* life? • Would you like to know the character? • Would you like to have a similar experience? • Who else would like this book? Why? • Is there another book that reminds you of this book in some way? How?	• What was your first impression of this book? • Did your impression change as you continued to read? • Overall, how do you rate this book? Why? • What was the best part of this book? • What surprised you? • What disappointed you? • What could the author have done to improve this book? • What made you keep reading?

BEFORE READING

- Activate prior knowledge
- Make predictions
- Set purpose (clarify the strategy application)
- Introduce vocabulary as appropriate
- Explain *how* to find the strategy (make the reading strategic)

DURING READING

- Model how you find the evidence
- Provide time for students to practice finding evidence—prompted or unprompted
- Apply other strategies as appropriate (without losing the focus of the lesson)
- Address vocabulary as needed

AFTER READING

- Reflect orally on the use of the strategy
- Provide written strategy follow-up task if appropriate

RUBRIC FOR USING INDIVIDUAL STRATEGIES ACCURATELY AND INSIGHTFULLY

	Accurate and Insightful	Accurate and Adequate	Inaccurate or Insufficient
Notice	Notices basic text elements during reading in order to comprehend; also sees small details that other readers may miss and recognizes their implications for meaning	Notices basic text elements during reading in order to comprehend	Frequently misses basic text elements which limits comprehension, including summarizing and retelling
Picture	Uses specific information in the text to describe an elaborate, multi-sensory mental image, inferring additional details to add to the context	Uses specific information in the text to describe a clear image that uses two or more senses	Uses background information rather than text details to create a mental image, or the image is very limited, or the student is unable to form *any* mental image
Wonder	Asks questions that probe the underlying, deep meaning of the text and lead to significant insights	Asks reasonable questions that demonstrate engagement with the text though the questions don't lead to significant insights	Questions are superficial or the reader is not engaged enough to ask any questions
Predict/ Guess	Predictions show attention to small details and the capacity to make inferences by synthesizing multiple pieces of information	Predictions are reasonable based on evidence in the text	Predictions are way off-base with little connection to textual evidence
Figure Out: Infer	Independently recognizes the message, theme, or main idea of the story beyond the lesson the character learns	Recognizes the message, theme, or main idea with teacher support; needs help moving from what the *character* learns to what the *reader* learns	Does not recognize the theme, message, or main idea of a text even with teacher support; very literal understanding at best
Figure Out: Synthesize	Easily synthesizes information in order to summarize it, including information from multiple sources	Synthesizes information into a summary, but the summary sometimes contains too many or too few details	Unable to put text elements together to derive an appropriate summary
Connect	Connects to the big idea or theme using personal examples different from those in the text and may even suggest a possible "action step" to apply the connection in a real-life situation	Connects to the big idea or theme of a text using personal examples different from those in the text	Connects to small, inconsequential details that are really just coincidences

CHECKLIST FOR USING INDIVIDUAL COMPREHENSION STRATEGIES

NAME: _____ **DATE:** _____

_____ 1.   I **notice** the important information when I am reading—even some details that other readers might not notice. I see how these details are important to the text.

_____ 2.   I can describe **pictures in my mind** as I read that include lots of details: what I see, hear, smell, etc.

_____ 3.   I ask very thoughtful questions as I read that show I am **wondering** about the problem, characters, or something else important in the text.

_____ 4.   I make **predictions** as I read that use information from the text and my background knowledge to anticipate what might happen next—and I can explain my reasons.

_____ 5.   I can **figure out** (infer) important ideas in a text, such as the theme or lesson without help from my teacher.

_____ 6.   I can **figure out** (synthesize) information in the text by putting the information together in a clear summary that is not a retelling.

_____ 7.   I can **connect** to the big idea or theme in the text by showing how this big idea has been important in my own life. I use examples to show this that are *different* from the author's examples.

AN EXAMPLE OF REALLY GOOD STRATEGY USE WAS WHEN

_____

_____

_____

INSTRUCTIONAL FOCUS: FLUENCY

What's the purpose?

The purpose of this instructional focus is for students to improve their oral reading fluency—beyond the too typical and much oversimplified emphasis on speed and accuracy only. While these two criteria are important, they are hardly enough to distinguish a reader who is truly fluent—one who also reads with attention to punctuation, appropriate phrasing, and good expression and who simultaneously demonstrates solid passage comprehension. The lessons proposed here for a small-group instructional focus on fluency feature use of punctuation, phrasing, expression, and smoothness as critical features of fluency that align with comprehension.

Who would benefit from this focus?

Students who miss the mark based on any of the criteria above are good candidates for small-group lessons with a fluency focus. Some common symptoms of poor fluency beyond rate and accuracy are reading that ignores punctuation or chunking of text into meaningful phrases and reading that is done in a flat, monotone voice devoid of expression or regard for the tone of the text. Some students who read in an uneven, choppy manner, sometimes moving smoothly through text and other times reading in a halting, start-and-stop fashion, would benefit from small-group instruction that focuses on fluency—*if* their lack of smoothness is a function of their lack of confidence. However, when the choppy, dysfluent reading is due to slow or inaccurate word recognition, students need instruction that treats the *causes* of that problem, not just the *symptoms*.

What kinds of texts should I use?

Texts that work well for fluency often contain language with the rhythms and cadences of natural speech. This includes, but is not limited to, poetry. It might also be narrative text that incorporates alliteration (*silver swimming swans*), a series of sentences that repeat a particular word pattern—with the final sentence breaking the pattern, made-up words (think: Dr. Seuss), etc. Also consider texts with dialogue in the voices of multiple speakers. "List" poems lend themselves to choral reading, a fun format for fluency practice. And, of course, plays and reader's theater scripts are perennial favorites and likewise provide performance opportunities, legitimizing in "kid thinking" the need for *practicing* oral reading. For informational text, I like to find passages that can be read aloud in the voice of a newscaster with an aura of authority and attention to emphasis of important content words.

What resources will I need for teaching and assessing?

- *Possible Fluency Focus Lessons* (for students who would benefit from a particular fluency focus), pages 136-138

- *Poems for Fluency Focus Lessons* (for poems suitable for practicing smoothness, punctuation, phrasing, and expression), page 139

- *Poems for Choral Reading* (for poems suitable for various choral speaking techniques), page 140

- *Fluency Rubric* (for the teacher to assess students' fluency), page 141

- *Fluency Checklist* (for students to assess their own fluency), page 142

How do I implement this?

Lessons on individual aspects of fluency are useful for students who demonstrate a particular weakness in one or more fluency components. Suggestions for how to implement lessons with these specific focus points are included in *Possible Fluency Focus Lessons* (pages 136-138) as a resource for teaching fluency. See the list of *Poems for Fluency Focus Lessons* (page 139) to support students' specific fluency needs. However, most intermediate-grade students who need continued focus on fluency will benefit most from lessons that integrate *all* fluency components. There's no shortage of appropriate text for practicing fluency (as noted previously: narrative and non-narrative text, reader's theater scripts, and poetry.) While all of these text types have merit and similar implementation steps that can be followed, I focus here on the use of poems and choral reading of poems, as I have found poetry to be a much overlooked text structure that is especially well suited to performance, and hence, repeated oral practice. Choral reading, similar to reader's theater, provides an authentic purpose for improving fluency. To use poetry to improve fluency:

1. Choose a relatively short poem with a strong rhythm. You may even be able to find poems that align with a particular curriculum topic or theme.

2. Copy the poem onto chart paper, or give each student a copy of his/her own.

3. Review the components of fluent reading, referring to the *Fluency Checklist* (page 142), which students should have in their reading folder or which should be posted in a larger format within easy view.

4. Read the poem *to* students—without rushing and with attention to smoothness, punctuation, phrasing, and expression.

5. Read the poem *with* students or "echo read"—first the teacher reads a line; then students repeat it, mimicking the teacher's smoothness, use of punctuation, phrasing, and good expression.

6. Read the poem together again if appropriate to get a general sense of the sound of it—and to talk about the poem's meaning.

7. Now look at individual lines and highlight features that contribute to fluency: Is there an exclamation point? A word written in italics? An "unmarked" word that just begs for emphasis? A portion of the text that should be read extra quietly or in a tone that conveys grief, excitement, or another emotion? A group of words that should be chunked together? Mark the text or, if students have their own copy, encourage them to mark it up as a reminder about how and where to apply particular aspects of fluency.

8. Reread individual lines, paying special attention to the fluency points you've noted. Read the lines in unison at first, and then let individual children try them alone if they wish to do so.

9. After completing the entire poem, students can go off to practice it alone or with a partner. Remind them about the criteria (see the *Fluency Checklist*) for all components of fluency.

10. "Perform" the poem the next day using one of the techniques described in the next section; ask students to reflect on their own fluency based on the criteria in the *Fluency Checklist*.

11. Add this poem to a growing repertoire of poems your students have read chorally. Return to it periodically to practice fluency but, most of all, to enjoy it. Kids *love* reading poems aloud in this way.

Kicked-up Choral Reading

Joining in on the refrain or a repeated line

- This poetry strategy requires that students learn about timing so they will jump in only when their lines come up (which makes choral reading a great opportunity to focus on listening as well as reading).

- Students still participate as a whole class for their given line or lines, with no pressure to speak individually.

- As always, the teacher reads the entire poem first. Then, in repeated readings, students join in on a line or refrain that pops up repeatedly in the poem. This is low pressure (hence, great for ELL) because all of the voices blend together.

- It can be helpful to write the word or phrase on a strip of paper and point to it as a visual cue when students take their turn.

Call and response

- Once students are familiar with poems read aloud, the teacher can divide the class in half to read poems in a call-and-response fashion.

- The best poems for this poetry strategy are those with lines structured in a kind of back-and-forth way. (Mary Ann Hoberman's series of poetry books, *You Read to Me, I'll Read to You*, is *perfect* for call and response.)

Multiple groups, multiple stanzas

- This is slightly more challenging than other choral reading strategies because it uses multiple small groups.

- This puts the focus on fewer students; thus, it takes more practice.

- Different groups read different stanzas.

- Be sure to pair English language learners or struggling students with students who are more confident and comfortable with reading aloud.

Solo lines

- List-like poems work well for solo lines.

- In poems such as these, individual voices read single lines.

- Most children enjoy the opportunity for solo lines, but be sure students are familiar with the poem before introducing the idea of solos.

- This is great practice for developing a sense of timing and for listening in order to know when it is your turn to speak.

- Work on making this type of reading like a performance, with attention to all fluency components.

How do I measure students' success?

A student's fluency should be measured using all of the fluency criteria on the *Fluency Rubric*.

- **Level 1:** Fluent reading that demonstrates reasonable pacing, smoothness, good phrasing, use of punctuation, and expression with developmentally appropriate text that is <u>below grade level</u>.

- **Level 2:** Fluent reading that demonstrates reasonable pacing, smoothness, good phrasing, use of punctuation, and expression with developmentally appropriate text that is <u>on grade level</u>.

- **Level 3:** Fluent reading that demonstrates reasonable pacing, smoothness, good phrasing, use of punctuation, and expression with developmentally appropriate text that is <u>above grade level</u>.

POSSIBLE FLUENCY FOCUS LESSONS

Providing students with copies of texts that they can mark up facilitates fluency instruction.

Phrasing

Show students how they can **group words** and read them in appropriate clauses or phrases. Phrasing often requires attention to prepositional phrases (*in the house; under the table*) or clauses (*although my room is small...*). In these cases, there is often no punctuation to guide the reader. Lines of poetry are good for this since the text is already broken into short segments which can be further divided into even shorter chunks if appropriate. A short narrative or non-narrative passage can also be used to teach phrasing. I advise children to draw a slash (/) mark to show where one group of words ends and the next begins. Or, they can "scoop" words that go together.

1. Read the poem or passage to students, or ask them to read it along with you. Be sure to include good phrasing, but don't exaggerate it too much.

2. Now go back and read one line or sentence at a time, deciding together how the words should be grouped. Students should mark their own text with scoops or slash marks to indicate appropriate phrases.

3. Read each line together, emphasizing the phrasing the group has determined.

4. Students may read the lines individually as well.

5. After working on two or three lines or sentences, go back and read them together until the phrasing sounds natural.

6. After completing the entire passage, students can go off to practice it alone or with a partner. Remind them about the criteria (see rubric) for good phrasing.

7. "Perform" the passage or poem individually, in pairs, etc. the next day, evaluating how well good phrasing contributes to fluency.

Punctuation

Show students how they can use punctuation to enhance fluency. Select a poem or short passage that incorporates various "interesting" punctuation marks beyond a simple period at the end of a sentence: exclamation point, comma, question mark, colon, semicolon, ellipses, etc.

1. Find the punctuation in the text and ask students to highlight each punctuation mark in some way, such as with a highlighter or by drawing a line underneath it. Talk about the role of each of the punctuation marks.

2. Read the passage to the students or have students read along. Your attention to each punctuation mark should be apparent, but not overly exaggerated.

3. Now go back and practice each line individually, paying special attention to the punctuation.

4. Students may then read the lines aloud by themselves or with a partner.

5. After working on a few lines or sentences, go back and read them all together, attending carefully to the punctuation.

6. After completing the entire passage, students can go off to practice it alone or with a partner. Remind them about the criteria (see rubric) for using punctuation.

7. "Perform" the passage or poem individually, in pairs, etc. the next day, evaluating how well attention to punctuation contributes to fluency.

Expression

Emphasizing particular words in a text, reading some parts loudly and others quietly, and changing your tone depending on which character in the story is speaking all contribute to expressive reading. Sometimes an author "directs" the reading of the text by writing some words in a **bold** font or writing a word in ALL CAPS. Or maybe the word is written in *italics*. In these cases, it's pretty easy to tell which words need to be read with greater emphasis. But other times, readers need to figure this out for themselves. Likewise, readers need to infer nuances in characters' perceived tone of voice so that when the passage or poem includes words spoken by a character or a conversation between two or more people, different characters sound different. The listener should be able to infer the intended mood of the message.

1. Choose a poem or passage with opportunities for expressive reading. These might include (but would not be limited to):

    - Poems or passages with bolded or italicized font, words written in uppercase letters, or words of varying font sizes

    - Poems or passages where one character speaks

    - Poems or passages where two or more characters engage in a conversation

    - Poems or passages that evoke strong emotions (anger, fear, joy, excitement, etc.)

2. Discuss what is included in expressive reading: reading different words or phrases differently to help convey the meaning of the text. Discuss how an author directs you to emphasize some words more than others.

3. Ask students to find any places in the text where the author wants the reader to add emphasis (or speak extra quietly).

4. Read the poem or passage to students, or ask them to read it along with you. Be sure to read expressively, but don't overdo it.

5. Identify the intended tone of the text. Is it upbeat and cheerful? Sad? Discouraged? Excited? Something else? Does the text represent different moods?

6. Read sentences/lines one at a time, determining which words should be emphasized and how they should be read.

7. Practice reading the lines together as a group and one student at a time until the whole passage can be read dramatically.

8. After completing the entire passage, students can go off to practice it alone or with a partner. Remind them about the criteria (see rubric) for reading with expression.

9. "Perform" the passage or poem individually, in pairs, etc. the next day, evaluating how well attention to expression contributes to fluency.

Smoothness

Students who read in an uneven, halting manner for reasons that don't reflect poor word-recognition skills may simply need to build their oral reading confidence in order to read more fluently. Choose easy text for these students. Choose text that includes vocabulary and sentence patterns that are familiar so that when students read, the language feels natural to them. Fiction generally approximates natural speech more readily than nonfiction. Feedback and encouragement are essential if we want improved confidence to improve fluency.

1. Read the text aloud to students, reminding them before you begin that you are going to try to read smoothly without hesitating before individual words. Focus on smoothness with enough expression to keep students engaged but not so dramatically that they are distracted from your main mission—the smoothness of your reading.

2. Read the text again with the students reading along. Read at a natural pace, but make sure that students can keep up.

3. Now look at the text one sentence/line at a time. Ask students to "rehearse" the line with a partner until their reading sounds like "regular talking."

4. As students master each new line, go back and read all previous lines to build stamina for fluent reading: Just keep going…

5. After completing the entire passage, students can go off to practice it alone or with a partner. Remind them about the criteria (see rubric) for reading smoothly.

6. "Perform" the passage or poem individually the next day, evaluating how well attention to smoothness contributes to fluency.

POEMS FOR FLUENCY FOCUS LESSONS

The following poems for both fluency focus lessons and choral reading come from books by Shel Silverstein and Jack Prelutsky that happen to be on my bookshelf. I chose them because these books might be on your bookshelf, too, and if not, they would be easy to find in your school library. Mostly, though, I chose these poems because these two authors make language fun! When you're working on fluency, it is so important to engage students with the words themselves. While the poems under each category will work well for a particular fluency focus or a choral reading technique, all of these poems would be wonderful for *all* aspects of fluency.

Expression

Listen to the Mustn'ts, Where the Sidewalk Ends by Shel Silverstein, page 27
Snowman, Where the Sidewalk Ends by Shel Silverstein, page 65
The Crocodile's Toothache, Where the Sidewalk Ends by Shel Silverstein, page 66
Ladies First, A Light in the Attic by Shel Silverstein, page 148
When Tillie Ate the Chili, The New Kid on the Block by Jack Prelutsky, page 88
Ma! Don't Throw That Shirt Out, The New Kid on the Block by Jack Prelutsky, page 120
I'm Disgusted with My Brother, The New Kid on the Block by Jack Prelutsky, page 128

Phrasing

Us, Where the Sidewalk Ends by Shel Silverstein, page 36
Spaghetti, Where the Sidewalk Ends by Shel Silverstein, page 100
Oh, Teddy Bear, The New Kid on the Block by Jack Prelutsky, pages 110-111
Deep in Our Refrigerator, It's Raining Pigs and Noodles by Jack Prelutsky, pages 62-63
Why Do I Have to Clean My Room?, It's Raining Pigs and Noodles, pages 102-103

Punctuation

For Sale, Where the Sidewalk Ends by Shel Silverstein, page 52
Melinda Mae, Where the Sidewalk Ends by Shel Silverstein, pages 154-157
Homework, The New Kid on the Block by Jack Prelutsky, pages 54-55

Smoothness

One Inch Tall, Where the Sidewalk Ends by Shel Silverstein, page 55
Tree House, Where the Sidewalk Ends by Shel Silverstein, page 79
The Flying Festoon, Where the Sidewalk Ends by Shel Silverstein, page 80
Dancing Pants, Where the Sidewalk Ends by Shel Silverstein, page 126
How Not to Have to Dry the Dishes, A Light in the Attic by Shel Silverstein, page 12
The Fly Is In, A Light in the Attic by Shel Silverstein, page 100
I'm Roaring Like a Lion, It's Raining Pigs and Noodles by Jack Prelutsky, page 66

POEMS FOR CHORAL READING

Joining in on the refrain or a repeated line

Peanut Butter Sandwich, Where the Sidewalk Ends by Shel Silverstein, pages 84-86

My Dog, He Is an Ugly Dog, The New Kid on the Block by Jack Prelutsky, pages 62-63

Today Is Very Boring, The New Kid on the Block by Jack Prelutsky, pages 96-97

I'm in a Rotten Mood Today, The New Kid on the Block by Jack Prelutsky, page 142

Call and response

The Fourth, Where the Sidewalk Ends by Shel Silverstein, page 15

Dreadful, Where the Sidewalk Ends by Shel Silverstein, page 141

How Many, How Much, A Light in the Attic by Shel Silverstein, page 8

Here Comes, A Light in the Attic by Shel Silverstein, page 32

One Two, A Light in the Attic by Shel Silverstein, page 102

I'm Thankful, The New Kid on the Block by Jack Prelutsky, pages 28-29

Multiple groups, multiple stanzas

Jimmy Jet and His TV Set, Where the Sidewalk Ends by Shel Silverstein, pages 28-29

Smart, Where the Sidewalk Ends by Shel Silverstein, page 35

Rock 'n' Roll Band, A Light in the Attic, pages 24-25

I Wonder Why Dad Is So Thoroughly Mad, The New Kid on the Block by Jack Prelutsky, page 11

I Am Falling Off a Mountain, The New Kid on the Block by Jack Prelutsky, page 149

Solo lines

Boa Constrictor, Where the Sidewalk Ends by Shel Silverstein, page 45

Hector the Collector, Where the Sidewalk Ends by Shel Silverstein, pages 46-47

Sick, Where the Sidewalk Ends by Shel Silverstein, pages 58-59

Sarah Cynthia Sylvia Stout Would Not Take the Garbage Out, Where the Sidewalk Ends by Shel Silverstein, pages 70-71

Recipe for a Hippopotamus Sandwich, Where the Sidewalk Ends by Shel Silverstein, page 115

Messy Room, A Light in the Attic by Shel Silverstein, page 35

The New Kid on the Block, The New Kid on the Block by Jack Prelutsky, page 7

Louder Than a Clap of Thunder, The New Kid on the Block by Jack Prelutsky, page 36

My Mother Says I'm Sickening, The New Kid on the Block by Jack Prelutsky, pages 112-113

I'm the Single Most Wonderful Person I Know, The New Kid on the Block by Jack Prelutsky

Today Was Not My Day at All, It's Raining Pigs and Noodles by Jack Prelutsky, pages 96-97

FLUENCY RUBRIC

STUDENT: _____ **DATE:** _____

	3 Excellent	2 Generally Good	1 Needs Work
Smoothness and pace	Reads smoothly at a conversational pace; quickly self-corrects any word-level difficulties	The reading is generally fluent with some hesitations and false starts that detract from smoothness and reduce pace	Frequent hesitations and false starts break the smoothness of the reading; much word-by-word, labored, and uneven reading
Punctuation	Consistently makes use of punctuation to enhance phrasing and expression	Attends to punctuation most of the time, but punctuation adds to phrasing and expression only minimally	Generally ignores punctuation to the detriment of both phrasing and expression
Phrasing	Reads with good phrasing, grouping words into meaningful chunks	Phrasing generally reflects adequate grouping of words, though some run-ons and extended pauses interfere with flow	There is no sense of phrase boundaries, resulting in awkward flow
Expression	Reads with good expression throughout the text; changes voice based on interpretation of the passage	Some reading is expressive; occasionally slips into expressionless reading.	Reading may be too quiet or nearly devoid of expression with no sense of natural speech

Smoothness: _____

Punctuation: _____

Phrasing: _____

Expression: _____

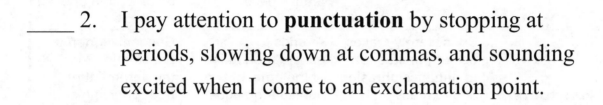

I am reading fluently if...

_____ 1. I read smoothly at a good **pace** (not too slow and not too fast; my reading is *not* choppy).

_____ 2. I pay attention to **punctuation** by stopping at periods, slowing down at commas, and sounding excited when I come to an exclamation point.

_____ 3. I get the **phrasing** right so my reading sounds like natural talking.

_____ 4. I use great **expression** so my voice makes the reading sound interesting (loud, soft, happy, sad, etc.).

INSTRUCTIONAL FOCUS: VOCABULARY

What's the purpose?

The purpose of vocabulary instruction is more complicated than it appears on the surface. The obvious answer to why we teach vocabulary is to increase students' word knowledge. Well, of course. But *what* words? *How many* words? Exactly *how* do these words impact comprehension? The teaching of vocabulary has gotten quite a bit of attention lately through the work of experts like Isabel Beck, Robert Marzano, and their colleagues.

Beck gave us the concept of "tiered" vocabulary. Tier One words are basically high-frequency words like *house* and *horse* and *baby* that most students except English language learners will probably know without actual instruction. Tier Three words are domain-specific terms such as those associated with a particular content area. (For example, some *tier three* geography words might be *isthmus, peninsula,* and *strait.*) Beck makes the claim that words such as these should not be the main focus of our vocabulary teaching as they do little to enhance students' everyday language. Instead, she would have us focus on Tier Two words. These are words that are useful to understanding the text. But even more significantly, they are words that students will use evermore to make their speaking and writing more powerful and their comprehension richer: *The little girl felt <u>dreadful</u> when she broke her mother's vase. Sam <u>charmed</u> the audience when he performed his magic trick. Dreadful* and *charmed* are words out of this week's small-group text that students will use again and again as they describe a situation orally or in writing.

I fully support the teaching of Tier Two words. But, in addition, I believe we also need to find a place for Tier Three, those domain-specific terms. Marzano calls this "academic vocabulary" and actually offers teachers lists of words that he thinks students should know at different developmental levels. This may be a bit too prescriptive, but the intent is valid: Kids *do* need to know the language associated with a wide range of topics and content areas—geography, the solar system, U.S. history, etc. And since social studies and science have gotten crowded out of the curriculum in so many classrooms, we really need to infuse this kind of vocabulary work into our teaching of informational text within our literacy instruction.

The purpose of our vocabulary instruction thus needs to be two-fold: to teach Tier Two words *and* to teach Tier Three words. (You will also need to pay attention to Tier One words for English language learners.) Both Beck and Marzano (as well as other experts on vocabulary instruction) offer substantial menus of possibilities for introducing and reinforcing vocabulary. Three of my favorite resources for the teaching of vocabulary are noted here with short annotations:

- Beck, I. L., McKeown, M. G. & Kucan, L. (2002). *Bringing words to life: Robust vocabulary instruction.* New York: Guilford Press.

  This little book explains Beck's three-tier vocabulary approach, complete with lots of practical, classroom-ready ideas for immediate implementation. If you have only one resource for teaching vocabulary, this should probably be it!

- Beck, I. L., McKeown, M. G. & Kucan, L. (2008). *Creating robust vocabulary: Frequently asked questions and extended examples*. New York: Guilford Press.

    This follow-up resource to the book above is my real favorite and the one I share with teachers in workshops and graduate classes. It begins with a substantial Q & A section—all those questions you still need answered about vocabulary instruction. There's also a chapter on English language learners, an extensive menu of good vocabulary activities, and a terrific chapter on professional development that lays out exactly how vocabulary instruction can be explained to teachers at all grade levels.

- Marzano, R. J. & Pickering, D. J. (2005). *Building academic vocabulary: Teacher's manual*. Alexandria, VA: Association for Supervision and Curriculum Development.

    This is actually the teacher's manual that accompanies another of Marzano's books, *Building Background Knowledge for Academic Achievement: Research on What Works in Schools*. I prefer this volume over the "real" book for thinking about vocabulary instruction because it focuses exclusively on the topic of vocabulary. It contains lots of practical suggestions without a great deal of narrative. It also includes close to one hundred pages of word lists targeting essential words at different levels in many content areas: health, civics, general history, etc.

My goal here is not to offer a list of vocabulary "activities," though teachers certainly need many strategies for maintaining words once they have been introduced. Instead, I want to describe two techniques I've been sharing with teachers for many years for enhancing students' Tier Two and Tier Three vocabulary. I call the Tier Two strategy *Vocabulary Connections*. If we want students to use new vocabulary in their speaking and writing, they need to see a connection between these words and their own lives. The Tier Three strategy is *Vocabulary Pyramid* and is especially useful for informational materials. This strategy calls for *synthesizing* new words so that they work *together*—an important factor in content-area knowledge. These strategies are applied most productively in small groups. Both are easily differentiated.

Who would benefit from this focus?

Nearly all children will benefit from attention to vocabulary, both Tier Two and Tier Three words. This becomes clear to us as we read their writing and listen to them talk. Their language is often sloppy, imprecise, and lacking the strong verbs, specific nouns, and clear description of students who have a stronger hold on the power of the spoken and written word. Of course, English language learners and students with language deficiencies have the greatest need for vocabulary work. But every kid in our class would have something to gain from *good* vocabulary instruction—instruction derived from connecting words to actual books, not workbooks. A focus on vocabulary would be a great comprehension enhancer and a nice addition to the instruction of any small group about once a week, maybe more for students whose vocabularies are especially limited.

What kinds of texts should I use?

It's important to have your students' vocabulary needs on your radar screen when you select texts for your small-group work. If there are no (or few) words rich enough to qualify as Tier Two or Tier Three vocabulary, maybe this isn't such a great resource. How many words should you choose? Anywhere from four to eight words could be appropriate based on the composition of your group. Four words will be plenty for younger or struggling students. More capable readers can handle six to eight words. If the text has more than eight (or so) words that you *could* use, eliminate a few that have the least potential for impacting your students' speaking and writing. If, however, the text has long lists of words that you anticipate your students do *not* know but *must* understand to comprehend the text—put the book back and find another one that contains less demanding vocabulary.

Here's another tricky matter that you need to consider, especially with regard to Tier Three words: Sometimes there are important concept words that are *about* the book but not actually *in* the book. For example, there are lots of short leveled texts related to the Underground Railroad. Most of these books don't contain the words *segregation, discrimination, prejudice,* etc. But, students' comprehension will be significantly enhanced if they can attach labels to the concepts the book is describing. So, you sometimes need to look beyond the words on the page when you choose vocabulary.

In a nutshell, the vocabulary you choose should meet these criteria:

- Words should be partially known but a bit beyond students' everyday experience. They may say, "Oh, I've *heard* that word, but I'm not sure what it means."

- Words should come from the text *or* be related to the text.

- Words should be important to the understanding of the reading selection.

- Words should be important to students' reading, writing, and speaking beyond the text.

What resources will I need for teaching and assessing?

- *Template for Vocabulary Connections or Vocabulary Pyramid*: *Words in Context* (for identifying vocabulary and creating your contextual sentences), page 148

- *Template for Vocabulary Connections: Student Activity* (for creating *Vocabulary Connection* prompts), page 150

- *Model for Vocabulary Connections: Student Activity* (an example of contextual sentences and connection prompts for Tier Two words), pages 149 and 151

- *Templates for Vocabulary Pyramid* (graphic organizers for creating your Tier Three vocabulary activity), pages 152-153

- *Model for Vocabulary Pyramid: Vocabulary in Context* (an example of contextual sentences for Tier Three words), page 154

- *Model Vocabulary Pyramid* (an example of a completed *Vocabulary Pyramid* activity for one book), pages 155-156

- **Rubric for Vocabulary Knowledge and Use** (for teachers to use to assess students' vocabulary knowledge and use), page 157

- **Checklist for Vocabulary Knowledge and Use** (for students to use to reflect on their own vocabulary knowledge and use), page 158

How do I implement this?

Implementing *Vocabulary Connections*

1. Select a reasonable number of words for a given reading selection (leveled book, chapter, poem, short story, etc.). Four to eight words would generally be appropriate.

2. Construct and duplicate a *Vocabulary Connections: Words in Context* sheet, writing a sentence using each word in a context that clearly conveys its meaning. (I try to take a sentence directly from the text if it conveys meaning; when it doesn't, I create my own, making sure to use the word the same way it's used in the text.)

3. Construct and duplicate a *Vocabulary Connections: Student Activity* sheet with prompts that require students to show how the new words apply to their own lives.

4. Discuss the contextual sentences and words individually with your small group to help students understand them. Be sure to give students opportunities to use each word orally. Provide oral practice with sentence stems if needed to help struggling students answer the questions in complete sentences.

5. As an instructional follow-up, ask students to complete the *Vocabulary Connections: Student Activity* sheet independently.

   - Answers should be written in COMPLETE SENTENCES.
   - Answers should contain THE NEW VOCABULARY WORD.

6. Sharing completed sentences during the next group session is a good way to spot check students' work.

7. Of course, you should assess all student work thoroughly after it has been completed.

8. This strategy is easily differentiated by varying the number of responses required by different students. (More capable students might be directed to respond to *all* of the vocabulary prompts; students who struggle with language might be asked to select just a few of the words and respond to those.)

Implementing *Vocabulary Pyramid*

1. Select a reasonable number of content words that are important to the topic. While there may seem to be *many* words, try to restrict yourself to those terms that are the *most* important or at least the most manageable to the students in your group. (Four to eight words will generally be plenty.)

2. Create a *Vocabulary Pyramid: Words in Context* sheet that will guide students toward an understanding of each term. Try to show how the word is actually used; don't just provide a definition.

3. Talk with students about each word and encourage them to use two or more words together (orally). This will help them understand how the words relate to each other.

4. As a follow-up activity, the most capable students can combine as many of the new words as possible into a meaningful paragraph. A more moderate task would be to combine approximately four words into two meaningful sentences. A basic task for the most limited students would be to use two of the words together in a sentence that demonstrates understanding of how the words work together. Be sure to *always* expect students to incorporate at least two new words as this is primarily a synthesizing task. Note that on the model of this activity (page 156), all three boxes have been filled in. Students, however, would complete a single box.

5. As in the *Vocabulary Connections* activity above, spot checking students' responses during the next small-group session will give you some insight into their level of comprehension.

6. Assess *all* students' responses when the work has been completed and offer specific feedback.

How do I measure students' success?

- **Level 1:** Uses new words accurately in speaking and writing during vocabulary lessons
- **Level 2:** Uses new words accurately in speaking and writing beyond the vocabulary lesson itself
- **Level 3:** Demonstrates deeper comprehension of a text or topic by using new vocabulary to articulate clear, insightful thinking

VOCABULARY CONNECTIONS OR VOCABULARY PYRAMID: WORDS IN CONTEXT

WORD BANK FOR _____

1. _____

2. _____

3. _____

4. _____

5. _____

6. _____

7. _____

WORD BANK FOR _Stray by Cynthia Rylant_

stray	grudgingly	distress
timidly	abandoned	

1. When I saw the dog just roaming around our backyard, I thought it might be a **stray**.

2. I put on my skates and approached the ice **timidly**, afraid I might fall.

3. Tom turned off the TV **grudgingly** and stomped upstairs to do his homework.

4. Jen's eyes were full of **distress** when she realized she had broken her mom's favorite vase.

5. The **abandoned** house has been empty for years.

 **VOCABULARY CONNECTIONS: STUDENT ACTIVITY**

NAME: _____ **DATE:** _____

WORD BANK FOR _____

```
┌─────────────────────────────────────────────────────────────┐
│                                                             │
│                                                             │
│                                                             │
│                                                             │
└─────────────────────────────────────────────────────────────┘
```

1. **Prompt:** _____
   Response: _____

   _____

2. **Prompt:** _____
   Response: _____

   _____

3. **Prompt:** _____
   Response: _____

   _____

4. **Prompt:** _____
   Response: _____

   _____

5. **Prompt:** _____
   Response: _____

   _____

6. **Prompt:** _____
   Response: _____

   _____

7. **Prompt:** _____
   Response: _____

   _____

NAME: _____ **DATE:** _____

WORD BANK FOR *Stray by Cynthia Rylant*

stray	**grudgingly**	**distress**
	timidly	**abandoned**

1. **Prompt:** What would you do if you found a <u>stray</u> dog in your yard?
   Response: _____

   _____

2. **Prompt:** What would you approach <u>timidly</u>?
   Response: _____

   _____

3. **Prompt:** What is one thing you do <u>grudgingly</u>?
   Response: _____

   _____

4. **Prompt:** When would your eyes be full of <u>distress</u>?
   Response: _____

   _____

5. **Prompt:** If your friend asked you to go into an <u>abandoned</u> house, what would you do? Why?
   Response: _____

   _____

VOCABULARY PYRAMID

WORD BANK FOR _____

**WRITE A SENTENCE
WITH <u>TWO</u>
VOCABULARY WORDS.**

**WRITE A PARAGRAPH WITH AT LEAST
TWO SENTENCES USING <u>THREE</u> OR
<u>FOUR</u> VOCABULARY WORDS.**

**WRITE A PARAGRAPH WITH AT LEAST
TWO SENTENCES USING <u>FIVE</u> OR MORE
VOCABULARY WORDS.**

NAME: _____ **DATE:** _____

Use <u>two</u> new vocabulary words in one good sentence about this topic.

```



```

Use <u>three or four</u> new vocabulary words in two good sentences about this topic.

```



```

Use <u>five or more</u> new vocabulary words in a good paragraph of two or
more sentences about this topic.

```



```

WORD BANK FOR *Events Leading Up to the Civil War*

territories	representatives	Missouri Compromise
abolitionists	fugitive	seceded

1. New **territories** formed as people moved into the West, though they hadn't become states yet.

2. Every state in the Union had **representatives** in Congress who tried to convince other lawmakers to support laws that would help their particular state.

3. The **Missouri Compromise** was considered a "compromise" because it was fair to both the northern and the southern states. So that there would be an equal number of slave and free states, Missouri entered the Union as a *slave* state, and Maine entered as a *free* state.

4. **Abolitionists** believed in abolishing (or getting rid of) slavery.

5. Runaway slaves were considered **fugitives**, and the law said they must be returned to their owners. People who helped **fugitive** slaves were sent to jail or had to pay a big fine.

6. Before Abraham Lincoln became president, South Carolina **seceded** (or withdrew) from the Union. That meant they were no longer considered part of the United States. Other states eventually **seceded**, too.

VOCABULARY PYRAMID

WORD BANK FOR *Events Leading Up to the Civil War*

| territories | representatives | Missouri Compromise |
| abolitionists | fugitive | seceded |

WRITE A SENTENCE WITH <u>TWO</u> VOCABULARY WORDS.

WRITE A PARAGRAPH WITH AT LEAST TWO SENTENCES USING <u>THREE</u> OR <u>FOUR</u> VOCABULARY WORDS.

WRITE A PARAGRAPH WITH AT LEAST TWO SENTENCES USING <u>FIVE</u> OR MORE VOCABULARY WORDS.

VOCABULARY PYRAMID (MODEL)

NAME: _____ **DATE:** _____

Use <u>two</u> new vocabulary words in one good sentence about this topic.

> Sometimes <u>abolitionists</u> tried to hide <u>fugitive</u> slaves so they could get to the North and have their freedom.

Use <u>three or four</u> new vocabulary words in two good sentences about this topic.

> South Carolina <u>seceded</u> from the Union because people in that state were afraid that the <u>abolitionists</u> would get rid of slavery once Abraham Lincoln became president. Maybe they were afraid their <u>representatives</u> wouldn't be able to protect their rights in Congress.

Use <u>five or more</u> new vocabulary words in a good paragraph of two or more sentences about this topic.

> <u>Representatives</u> made the <u>Missouri Compromise</u> because they wanted to be fair to all <u>territories</u> that were becoming states. They couldn't stop South Carolina from <u>seceding</u> from the Union, though, because people there were afraid that <u>abolitionists</u> would take the side of <u>fugitive</u> slaves and try to get rid of slavery.

RUBRIC FOR ASSESSING VOCABULARY KNOWLEDGE AND USE

NAME: _____ DATE: _____

	3	2	1	0
Infers word meaning from context				
Defines a term in his/her own words				
Uses a new word in a sentence that shows meaning and makes sense				
Makes an effort to use new words to communicate ideas in speaking and writing				
Recognizes the significance of words in relation to important concepts (segregation, immigration, etc.)				
Uses vocabulary to discuss text elements in summarizing and retelling				
Uses vocabulary in oral and written responses to comprehension questions				
Classifies and categorizes words				
Enjoys knowing words and playing with words				

3 = beyond grade-level expectations; **2** = meets grade-level expectations; **1** = working toward grade-level expectations; **0** = not evident at this time

Comments: _____
_____
_____
_____
_____
_____

VOCABULARY CHECKLIST

NAME: _____ **DATE:** _____

_____ 1. I am good at figuring out the meaning of a new word when I see one in a sentence.

_____ 2. I am good at explaining/defining new vocabulary in my own words. (I don't just read the definitions from the dictionary.)

_____ 3. I am good at using new words in sentences that make sense.

_____ 4. I work hard to use new words in my speaking AND in my writing.

_____ 5. I am good at explaining the importance of a particular word to a topic or text.

_____ 6. I am good at using new vocabulary when I retell or summarize a story.

_____ 7. I am good at using new vocabulary when I write answers to open-ended comprehension questions.

_____ 8. I am good at classifying words into groups that make sense.

_____ 9. I enjoy learning new words and finding ways to use them.

Here's something I'm really good at when it comes to learning and using new words: _____

_____

_____

I could improve my understanding and use of new vocabulary by

_____

_____

_____

INSTRUCTIONAL FOCUS: AUTHOR'S CRAFT

What's the purpose?

The purpose of this instructional focus is to connect reading and writing by examining the craft within a piece of writing. There is much that we do as teachers to refine reading skills and strategies by helping students read like a good reader. This instructional focus will help students read like a writer. Getting good at identifying well-crafted places within a text will not only enhance comprehension, it will also provide great models for students' own writing (though transfer to writing is not the primary goal of this instructional focus). To make this easier and provide a context for crafts, they have been identified under the writing trait with which they are aligned. A writing trait is the broad category; an author's craft is one specific application of a trait.

Who would benefit from this focus?

This might not be the first thing you teach students because there are skills and strategies more central to comprehension than author's craft. However, this is a whole new lens through which to view reading and *all* children seem to enjoy finding the crafts that authors have embedded—once they know what they're looking for. The problem is that except for a few obvious crafts—similes, descriptive words, strong verbs, etc.—much of the actual craft in a text is overlooked because we (teachers!) don't really know what we're looking for either. This can be easily remedied. (See the *Author's Craft* charts on pages 162-163). Small-group lessons on author's crafts can also be used as a means of launching focused writing lessons.

What kinds of texts should I use?

A focus on author's craft is most productive if you revisit a text on the second or even third day for it is a way to examine it more deeply after constructing basic meaning or refining a particular comprehension skill or strategy. Even so, this will not be effective with all texts because some—especially lots of those little leveled books we use for small-group instruction—do not contain an abundance of good writing. Only choose this focus when you have a worthy text. You will know you have one because you will find several examples of a single craft throughout the book—if you want to focus on one craft. Or, you will find many different crafts in the same book—if you want to demonstrate how an author weaves together lots of good writing techniques in a single piece of writing. Again, reference the charts on pages 162-163 so you'll know what you're looking for.

What resources will I need for teaching and assessing?

- *Author's Craft: Find It in a Book* (a list of crafts within each of the writing traits to teach students), pages 162-163

- *Monitoring My Thinking about Writing Traits When I Read* (a follow-up task for students to reflect on the writing traits present within a text), page 164

- *Author's Crafts to Find in My Reading* (a task sheet to clarify for students the crafts they should look for in today's reading), page 165

- *How to Explain Writing Traits to Students* (a simple explanation of the writing traits for teachers to use with students), page 166

- *Rubric for Assessing a Student's Understanding of Author's Crafts* (for teachers to assess students), page 167

- *Checklist for Author's Crafts* (for students' self-reflection), page 168

How do I implement this?

When you're teaching about one specific craft

1. Choose the trait.

2. Choose a craft within the trait.

3. Find a text on students' instructional level that demonstrates the craft (preferably in lots of places).

4. **Explain** the craft to students.

5. Think aloud about (**model**) the craft in one or two places.

6. Ask students to find other examples of the craft in this text.

7. Later: Provide opportunities for students to practice the craft in a specific writing task.

8. Later: Encourage students to use the craft in drafting or revising their own writing.

When you want students to identify a variety of specific crafts or general writing traits

1. Select a text that is well written, where many specific crafts or general traits are evident.

2. Review the crafts/traits with students that you want them to identify in the text. (Use the template, *Finding Author's Crafts in My Reading*, to indicate the specific crafts you want students to look for today or the template *Monitoring My Thinking about Writing Traits When I Read*.)

3. Ask students to use sticky notes or note in some other way where they located the identified crafts/traits. This may be done during the group session or independently as a follow-up task.

4. Share evidence after reading or during a follow-up session.

How do I measure students' success?

Although students' understanding of author's crafts is usually measured through their *writing*, remember that the standard here is more focused on *reading*. It is possible to consider the transfer of crafts from reading to writing as a very high level of performance in this context, but it would not be fair to expect that of all students or even fairly strong students. Instead, the primary gauge needs to be students' capacity to recognize the components of a well-crafted text and to understand how these crafts enhance the writing.

- **Level 1:** Identifies one or two crafts present within a text that make it a well-crafted piece of literature

- **Level 2:** Identifies a range of crafts present within a text that make it a well-crafted piece of literature and explains how these crafts make the writing more powerful

- **Level 3:** Meets the Level 2 standard and independently applies crafts learned in reading to his/her own writing

AUTHOR'S CRAFTS FOR DEVELOPING AND REFINING AN <u>IDEA</u>

Developing an idea
- Writing "small" (small details) to *show* rather than *tell*
- Snapshot of a person or place
- Thoughtshots—thoughts in the character's head (internal dialogue)
- A line of dialogue that shows *character*
- Gestures

Refining an idea
- Lots of details to support the topic
- The most exciting part of a story is the biggest part; an event in slow motion
- Unusual details
- Clearly identified main ideas and details
- Notice small details that use all of your senses

AUTHOR'S CRAFTS FOR DEVELOPING <u>VOICE</u>

- The author sounds like s/he knows a lot about the topic
- The text is written with language that a real kid would use
- Authors and characters have *attitude*
- The text is written from the point of view of something that doesn't talk (like a truck or a tree)
- An unexpected point of view (like the story is told from the wolf's point of view)
- Written in dialect
- Written directly to "you"
- Written in two or more voices
- Sounds humorous

AUTHOR'S CRAFTS FOR ENHANCING <u>WORD CHOICE</u>

- Specific color words, size words, texture words, etc.
- Great action words
- Describing words used in interesting or unexpected ways
- Exaggeration
- Similes or other comparisons
- Interesting character names
- Made-up words
- Play on words
- Figurative language
- Proper nouns
- Personification

AUTHOR'S CRAFTS FOR ENHANCING FLUENCY

- There is more than one sentence on a topic and they are organized to move smoothly from one sentence to the next
- A long sentence is made from two short sentences
- Interesting sentence construction
- The sentences are different lengths—including very long and very short sentences
- The same starting sound is used for multiple words in a sentence (alliteration)
- There are repeated lines or phrases
- A variety of transition words are used
- Sentence fragments are used artfully
- *And* is used artfully to begin a sentence

AUTHOR'S CRAFTS FOR ORGANIZING A PIECE OF WRITING

All the necessary parts
- Beginning includes characters, "setup," problem; middle includes attempts and complications; end includes resolution, ending
- Ideas that are grouped together because they go together
- Interesting titles
- A problem/solution story (not a personal narrative)
- A clear sequence (like a personal narrative or a how-to)
- A great beginning
- An interesting ending

Different organizational structures
- Letter or journal
- Poem
- Framing question text
- Photo journal
- Alphabet book
- Memoir/personal narrative
- Story within a story
- Cumulative text
- A text pattern that changes at the end
- Circular texts
- Flashback

AUTHOR'S CRAFTS FOR ENHANCING CONVENTIONS AND PRESENTATION

These are added for effect:
- Exclamation marks
- Capital letters
- Bold letters
- Italics
- Parentheses
- Colons
- Interesting placement of print

NAME: _____ **DATE:** _____

TITLE OF BOOK: _____

## Ideas The author of this book had a really good writing idea. The idea was	## Organization This book had a great beginning because This book had a great ending because I like the way the author put this story together because
## Voice The author made this writing sound happy, funny, sad, excited, etc. by	## Word Choice Here are some of my favorite words or sentences in this writing: I like these words or sentences because
## Fluency This writing sounds good when you read it out loud because	## Conventions and Presentation The author got me to pay extra attention to some of the words by

AUTHOR'S CRAFTS TO FIND IN MY READING

Definition:

Definition:

Definition:

Definition:

Definition:

Definition:

Notice what the author did to make the writing interesting and fun to read:

- Notice the author's **idea** for this story and how s/he developed it.

- Notice how the author put the story together **(organization)**.

- Notice the tone of **voice** that the author uses: Is it happy, sad, excited, angry?

- Notice the great **words** the author uses that make a picture in your mind.

- Notice what makes the writing sound good when it's read out loud **(fluency)**.

- Notice the way the author uses punctuation and the way the author makes certain words stand out **(conventions and presentation)**.

RUBRIC FOR ASSESSING A STUDENT'S UNDERSTANDING OF AUTHOR'S CRAFTS

STUDENT'S NAME: _____ GRADE: _____ DATE: _____

	Excellent = 2	Developing = 1	Needs attention = 0
Recognizes author's crafts	Recognizes a wide range of author's crafts in texts across all writing traits	Recognizes a few (mostly common) author's crafts in texts within various writing traits	Recognizes very few—or no—author's crafts in texts
Explains the impact of author's crafts on a piece of writing	Easily articulates how a particular craft has enhanced a piece of writing	With teacher support, explains how a particular craft makes writing stronger	Seems to have no concept of how author's crafts enhance writing
Applies author's crafts in own writing*	Independently incorporates individual author's crafts into own writing after identifying them in literature models	Occasionally attempts to include crafts in own writing that have been identified through literature models	Doesn't recognize correlation between crafts in literature models and possibilities for including crafts in own writing

*Optional

NOTES ABOUT THIS STUDENT:

Areas of strength:

_____

_____

_____

Areas of need:

_____

_____

_____

CHECKLIST FOR AUTHOR'S CRAFTS

NAME: _____ **DATE:** _____

1. _____ I know a lot of author's crafts and I can find them when I read.

2. _____ I can explain how a particular author's craft that I spot in a text can make the writing better.

3. _____ I try to use author's crafts in my writing that I have learned about in reading.

Here's an author's craft that I'm good at finding when I read:

_____

_____

_____

_____

_____

I'd like to improve my understanding of author's crafts by

_____

_____

_____

_____

_____

Chapter Six

Extending Literacy Learning Through Discussion

More and more, I find myself talking to teachers about bringing *talk* back into their classrooms. Oh, kids do plenty of talking, teachers remind me. But are they talking seriously about the books they read? Are they discussing the great themes of literature? Are they thinking strategically and "outside the box" to cultivate their creative thinking and hone their capacity to think deeply about what they read?

Deep thinking is hard, teachers are quick to point out. Yes, identifying a theme (for example) is harder than some other reading tasks such as identifying a problem in a story or a fact in informational text. The problem and the fact are right there on the page. The theme is an abstraction that is inferred when you understand the problem or the facts or other basic elements of a text. The bigger issue here, however, is that kids have too few opportunities to explore theme and other higher-level concepts in their reading because we honestly don't teach reading very thematically anymore; we don't pursue higher-level thought beyond what is tested.

With so much emphasis currently on standards, accountability, and using student assessment data, we've tightened up our teaching and learned to be more focused in our delivery of instruction—which is all good. This *does* help students master standards that are tested. But we have simultaneously strayed too far from the "big ideas" that make learning relevant to children: *What does this book say to me? How will it change my thinking about how I view and interact with my world?* If we want deeper text-to-self connections, maybe should begin with texts that students genuinely care about.

When I share this thought with teachers, I feel compelled in the same breath to reinforce the continuing need for our clearly focused, explicit literacy instruction: this does *not* mean we get to go back to that place where "reading" was comprised of a bunch of book projects that might have been fun for kids but didn't produce any actual learning! So if we're not going to spend three weeks making and sewing a wardrobe for a larger-than-life cardboard cutout of Sarah (*Plain and Tall*), what *will* we do beyond teaching students the skills and strategies of good readers? (FYI: my daughter's "Sarah" still resides in our attic, where each year when I retrieve the Christmas ornaments, I pay homage to her now-faded calico housedress, a reminder of the multiple trips I made to the fabric store many years ago so Caitlin could complete her "character study" project.)

We need to teach students to *use* their skills to talk about the books they read and, in the process, delve deeper into meaning. But talking about text is tricky business, requiring the perfect alignment of several stars simultaneously:

- a text that really speaks to students
- questions that generate genuine conversation as well as deep thinking
- Interaction among students

Let's step into two classrooms to see what happens when all of the stars *do* align.

CLASSROOMS WHERE DISCUSSIONS WORKED

Ms. L.'s class
In the first class, a fourth grade, Ms. L. asked students to pull their chairs together in the front of the room. They were midway through a short chapter book where the main character had just lied in order to achieve some noble goal. The question was: *Was it okay for this character to lie given the circumstances?* Ms. L. asked children to consider their opinion for a moment and then respond orally. Two students replied that yes, it was okay for the character to lie; the remaining three decided no, the character's lie was not justified.

"Now try to convince each other that your point of view is the correct one," Ms. L. directed. Students on either side of the issue changed seats to huddle with their like-minded group-mates. Animated buzz followed as they flipped through their books, finding the evidence they needed to defend their case.

"So who wants to go first?" the teacher asked, pulling the group back together. The debate began: Point—counterpoint…Well…I think…No way, can't you see that…?"
"Can you reach a consensus?" Ms. L. interrupted. Time was running out. She returned to the students' initial opinions, which she had posted on the white board. Four children now concluded definitively that the lie had been justified; the fifth child agreed—reluctantly.

Ms. R.'s class
Now, a virtual visit to Ms. R.'s fifth grade. I have to pinch myself periodically when I visit Ms. R.'s room lately because three years ago, when I first stepped into this class, small-group instruction didn't exist—in any form. "These kids can't do this. I can't do this. I don't have the right resources. I don't even have the right furniture." The list of excuses was endless. I did a lot of modeling that year, and Ms. R. did put into practice some of the small-group strategies we discussed during our coaching sessions. I saw them when I went back for follow-up visits. But I didn't honestly believe that when I walked out of her classroom and closed the door, that any of those good practices were occurring until the next time I visited.

Fast forward to my most recent visit. Students' desks are pushed together in groups of four. The teacher is standing at the front of the class reviewing the routines that will prevail when the groups convene momentarily. The question relates to *Shiloh,* Newbery Medal-winning story by Phyllis Reynolds Naylor: *Was Marty justified in hiding Shiloh from Judd Travers?* I move from group to group, watching the conversation unfold. Everyone is talking. There is a system of chips that students push toward the person to whom they are responding: "I agree with...I would like to add...I don't think you can support that view because..." Apparently, the trick was to end the session with only a single chip on your desk, demonstrating that you responded to multiple speakers. I never quite caught on to the way this works, but the kids were on a roll, much too busy with their thinking to pause to explain the process to some random classroom visitor. Later, debriefing with the teacher, principal, and literacy coach, I suggested that they share the good things that were happening in this fifth grade with other intermediate-grade teachers in the school, perhaps even teachers throughout the district. How far this teacher has come in three years!

Why these discussions worked

The stars did align for these groups, yielding authentic discussion. Why? First, the text was familiar to students. They'd been reading these books for a while and had already constructed basic meaning for the current chapters. The main characters in both of these stories were children approximately the age of the students in these grades and they faced situations to which the students could readily relate. Second, the questions were potentially controversial, raising ethical issues that were debatable. Third, the teachers moved past inquisition (just asking questions). They even moved past engagement (getting all students to care), finding ways to get children to *interact*. You don't have a discussion until you have interaction!

In the case of Ms. L. in the fourth grade, the "debate" format made each child's voice important to the group process and simultaneously minimized the impact of her own voice. (It's so hard to generate a "real" discussion when the teacher weighs in early with her opinion: Isn't the teacher *always* right?) Furthermore, aiming for consensus raises the stakes for presenting a solid argument (and I did suggest this to this teacher beforehand). But once I saw this in action, I had second thoughts. No child should ever feel pressured by her peers to acquiesce on a strongly held personal belief solely to reach a unanimous decision. It's okay to hold tight to a dissenting view as long as you can justify that view with evidence from the text and a well-reasoned personal philosophy.

Ms. R.'s fifth-grade small-group discussion appeared easy and effortless; the teacher wasn't even part of any group. But like most things in the classroom that go well and seem simple, this discussion followed several lead-up lessons in which routines were set and procedures established. These fifth graders knew the language of discussion ("I agree," "I disagree," "I'd like to add to what you said..."). There was a system in place to hold them accountable to participating in the conversation (those chips I never quite got the hang of). Additionally, students were comfortable talking to each other—no worries that an opinion would be mocked by their peers for being "silly."

NANCY'S SHORT LIST OF CRITERIA FOR A GOOD DISCUSSION

Based on the previous two vignettes and many more that I have visited where discussion flourished and discussion floundered, here are a few pointers I suggest to teachers for getting a discussion started and keeping it moving:

- **Choose a fiction text that is close to children's experience or a nonfiction selection on a timely topic for which they have sufficient background knowledge and consider themselves stakeholders.** Can they imagine themselves in the character's shoes? Can they envision themselves facing a similar problem? Do they care about the topic and have a vested interest: the use and misuse of videogames, impact of pollutants on the environment, healthy/unhealthy cafeteria lunches? You can talk about and construct basic meaning around *any* topic—Greek gods, the construction of the Statue of Liberty, the geography of India—but you may not get much of a discussion going if students don't feel they have anything unique to contribute to these topics.

- **Choose an issue to discuss that could be viewed as controversial or debatable.** Good question: *Do you support the use of wind turbines?* Not-so-good question: *What are wind turbines used for?* In the case of the first question, there's plenty to debate. This is a hot topic currently, and students with enough background knowledge will surely line up on one side or the other. In the case of the second question (which is also open ended), students could retrieve evidence from the text and articulate it. But other than prompting for more details, your text talk won't feel like very much of an actual conversation.

- **Establish a process for interacting and a safe environment for that interaction to take place.** Ms. L. got a "debate" going. Ms. R.'s students used chips to track their interaction. Other less "formal" processes could have been equally effective. What was essential here was that both groups had learned the language of literature response and used that language fluidly to communicate with other group members. Similarly, both teachers had identified clear ground rules for respectful interaction among peers.

- **Construct basic meaning first—and THEN discuss.** When students come together to really talk about a text, they shouldn't be sorting out basic text elements: story characters, the problem, the solution, or the main idea and supporting details in nonfiction text. That should have happened "yesterday." Discussion is a means of moving comprehension to a deeper level. This is frequently a concern for me when I model group discussion: I arrive on the classroom scene and, in the space of twenty to thirty minutes, need to introduce a text, get kids to read it, and then talk about it meaningfully—presuming I can somehow instantly establish the kind of trust that will encourage kids to talk at all! (Most often, I resort to short, powerful poems as the foundation of our discussions. At least that minimizes the reading time.)

- **Prepare several questions because you can never tell which one(s) will really catch students' attention.** Sometimes you need to toss out a couple of "test questions" to get a feeling for what students want to talk about today. The first question I ask typically generates only moderate interest, even if it's an excellent question, because students need to get into their discussion groove. The next question and the one after that lead to the best talk. And don't be afraid to veer a bit off center when students' side questions (still related to the text) take you in a direction different from the questions you've painstakingly designed.

- **Have fun!** Preparing for your good discussion will take some work, but the discussion itself should be fun. The most important message we can communicate in any literature discussion is not the theme of the text or which point of view is the most defensible or anything else related to the content of the selection, but that talking together about what we read is a lot of fun. When someone in your group asks, "Can we do this again tomorrow?" your discussion has succeeded.

MOVING AHEAD WITH DISCUSSION

Beyond these simple guidelines, how do we move forward with small-group instruction that focuses on discussion? The texts and the techniques to get the conversation going are pretty much up to you, the classroom teacher. You know your kids, what they like to read, and how to keep them talking. (In the Introduction to Part II of this book, I do provide you with some suggestions for quality short texts that might add to your repertoire of resources appropriate for all small-group instructional formats: constructing basic meaning, skill and strategy reinforcement, and discussion.)

What I can offer you, however, are various protocols for questioning, each with its own emphasis:

- Do you want to give students continued practice with the kinds of questions they're likely to encounter on their state assessment? Use the ***A-D Strand Questions*** (pages 106-109) matched to the objectives you introduced in shared reading and reinforced in small-group lessons that emphasize strategy and skill building. These coordinate with the lessons in *Launching RTI Comprehension Instruction* and the response templates in *That's a GREAT Answer.*

- Do you want to extend thinking through the application of comprehension strategies? Use the resources for ***Talking Strategically about Text*** (pages 186-189) to address applications of particular strategies in an oral context. The same strategy prompts can also be used later in a reader's notebook to get that same thinking onto paper. (Coincidentally, many of these responses also meet state reading standards—but in more authentic ways than the very focused *A-D Strand Questions* mentioned above.)

- Do you want students to recognize that they can think more analytically and critically—"outside the box"—about their reading? For this, use ***Thinking Outside the Box*** (pages 191-192), where boxes that represent six different "reading lenses" become icons for the diverse ways that readers can respond to text.

- Do you want to focus specifically on questions for nonfiction reading (informational text)? Use ***Facing Facts: Questions for Informational Text*** (pages 196-199). Here you'll find questions that help students connect personally to content-area materials—not just what they *think*, but how they *feel* about what they read.

- Do you want to provide students with opportunities for creative thinking and responding to their reading beyond traditional written answers? Use ***Change It Up: Questions and Tasks for Creative Thinking*** (pages 201-204) to extend meaning beyond the words on the page. These questions can be explored initially during discussion and then applied by students individually through the completion of thoughtful creative-thinking tasks about their reading.

Welcome to the crazy quilt of discussion options. There's something for everyone here. The overriding purpose of each of these protocols is to improve students' capacity to talk about text in order to achieve deeper understanding of what they read. The particular protocol you choose on a particular day will reflect the means you've selected to attain that goal.

To streamline your use of the materials in this chapter, please reference resources related to **discussions in general** in the opening pages of this chapter: *What's the purpose? Who would benefit from this focus? What kinds of texts should I use? What resources will I need for teaching and assessing discussion? How do I implement this? How do I measure students' success?*

QUESTIONS TO CONSIDER

1. How often do you focus on *discussion* with your small groups (rather than *constructing meaning* or *reinforcing skills and strategies*)?

2. What are the problems your students typically encounter with discussions? How have you addressed these problems?

3. What do you think might contribute to better small-group discussions?

4. What questions do you hope the remainder of this chapter will answer for you?

INSTRUCTIONAL FOCUS: DISCUSSION

What's the purpose?

The purpose of this instructional focus is to build students' capacity to actively participate in a book discussion while also helping them comprehend more deeply. Note that the purpose of this focus is *not* written response—although students may subsequently respond in writing to open-ended questions or to prompts in a reader's notebook. For the most part, students will write answers to open-ended comprehension questions through whole-class shared-reading lessons and small-group lessons focused on specific comprehension objectives. Sometimes we just have to let kids talk!

Who would benefit from this focus?

All students need the opportunity to talk about text. Discussion promotes student interaction, a critical factor in comprehension. Too many students are very passive readers; it's hard to understand what you read when you're not really engaging with the words on the page. We often hear about the importance of "engagement," but what does engagement *look like*? It looks like kids interacting—talking to each other, maybe even arguing with each other, sticking to their position until they've persuaded their peers that their "side" is the right one. Or maybe one of their peers is more convincing, and that changes their perspective.

Discussing a variety of questions gives students continuous practice with multiple ways of viewing a text. This is helpful for students reading on or above grade level who don't need a lot of explicit instruction on individual objectives but who can certainly benefit from exposure to all kinds of angles from which to view their reading. For capable readers (with the assessment data to support this claim), the largest proportion of small-group time should be devoted to an instructional focus centered on discourse. In fact, asking students to respond orally to questions about a text can pinpoint specific comprehension objectives that need more explicit attention. For less proficient readers, small-group time should be divided between discourse and developing the literacy skills that will support powerful conversation about text: *constructing basic meaning* and *reinforcing skills and strategies*.

What kinds of texts should I use?

For this instructional focus, the length of the text is less critical than its quality. A chapter from a chapter book works well, or a nonfiction article, or a short story, or a poem. Although I have encountered a few leveled texts that I would deem worthy of a great discussion, too many of these little books (often the fictional variety) just don't measure up against the books and stories by "real" authors—the ones available to us on the shelves of our school or classroom library. Nonfiction leveled books, in my view, tend to be better. The topics are often timely. The graphics are sharp and pique students' interest. And there are abundant text features (table of contents, glossary, index, etc.) to support comprehension. Whatever text you choose, make sure you design questions that truly probe the depths of students' thinking.

If you fall back on questions you've asked about a favorite text for years and years, you'll be asking mostly literal-level questions that miss many of the most important ways that readers can reflect on their reading.

What resources will I need for teaching and assessing discussion?

Some resources are generic and apply to *all* of the discussion protocols. They are included in the list below. Others are specific to individual discussion formats and can be found later in this chapter where each protocol is more fully described.

- *Ways to Have a Good Discussion* (discuss and post these helpful guidelines to keep students talking in a discussion), page 178

- *Literature Discussion Prompts* (for building students' capacity to talk about text; post these near your small-group reading area and refer to them often as you teach students to build on each other's ideas, respectfully disagree, etc.), page 179

- *Rubric for Examining Teachers' Expertise in Leading a Discussion* (Teachers should reflect on their capacity to elicit student discourse. Or, this rubric can be used by literacy coaches or administrators when helping teachers to improve their classroom discussions about a text), page 180

- *Discussion Rubric for Assessing Student Discourse* (Teachers can assess students' discussion skills using these criteria), page 181

- *Checklist for Reflecting on Discussion Skills* (Students can reflect on their own discussion skills using the same criteria as in the rubric above—but in a simplified format), page 182

How do I implement this?

1. While a discussion around open-ended questions can be a stand-alone focus for a particular text, this small-group format frequently follows a lesson for *constructing basic meaning* or *reinforcing skills and strategies*. Students may reread the text to prepare for the discussion or simply reflect on their reading from the previous day.

2. The teacher should prepare a list of questions beforehand relative to a portion of text that can reasonably be discussed in one group session. The *Discussion Planner for Comprehension Strategies* suggests two questions for each strand or strategy. However, this is only a suggestion; even if the list includes eight questions, students might ultimately discuss fewer of them depending on the depth of the conversation.

3. You can give students the questions beforehand or wait until the group meets to present them. Either way can work. One advantage of distributing the questions prior to the group meeting is that students will have an opportunity to prepare their responses. "Prepare" doesn't have to mean "write." In fact, I think it is preferable for students to simply jot a few notes to remind them of their thinking with the expectation that they will elaborate more fully when they share their thoughts orally in the group.

4. Ask students to read the portion of text that will be discussed (with or without distributing the questions). Depending on the complexity of the text, you may or may not wish to do a lesson prior to your discussion that builds background: a lesson focused on the basic construction of meaning or a lesson on a specific comprehension objective—or both.

5. Bring the group together to respond orally to the questions. Remember that the goal of this focus is not just for students to develop higher-level thinking about a text, but to learn to interact more fully in a discussion. To that end, teachers also need to teach the art of discourse. Use the guidelines for *Ways to Have a Good Discussion* and *Literature Discussion Prompts* to help with this.

6. Optional: To further reinforce their thinking, students can also be asked to respond in writing to one of the questions. Note: *ONE* of the questions! We dilute the power of written response when we ask students to crank out response after response. For the purposes of this task, students can respond to a question *they* have selected (preferable). Or, the teacher can do the choosing.

How do I measure students' success?

Respectful and engaged participation in the discussion based on:

Level 1: Teacher-prompted responses that reveal deep thinking about a text

Level 2: Unprompted responses that demonstrate students' deep thinking and capacity to build on each other's ideas with a teacher guiding the discussion

Level 3: Unprompted responses that demonstrate students' deep thinking and capacity to build on each other's ideas with a peer acting as the discussion facilitator

1. Be prepared!

2. Sit so everyone can see each other.

3. Get started right away.

4. Look at the person who is talking.

5. Listen with an open heart.

6. Ask questions to understand better.

7. Speak clearly but not too loudly.

8. Wait for the speaker to finish.

9. Signal when you want a turn.

10. Be sure everyone gets a turn.

11. Build on each other's ideas.

12. Respect each other's ideas.

13. Stay on the topic.

14. Provide evidence for your thinking.

- I agree with _____ because....

- I agree with _____ but would like to add....

- I see it differently than _____ because....

- That's a good point, however....

- I hear what you're saying, but how about...?

- I'm confused about....Could you explain...?

- So, [name], what you mean is....

- Can you give me another example of...?

- What if...?

- [Name], what do you think about...?

- Have you ever thought about...?

- Adding on to what you are saying,....

- Are you sure? What makes you say/think that?

- For example,....

- I respectfully disagree with _____ because....

- What in the text makes you think...?

RUBRIC FOR EXAMINING TEACHERS' EXPERTISE IN LEADING A DISCUSSION

NAME: _____ DATE: _____

Criteria	2	1	0
The teacher asks questions that are well matched to the text across different thinking strands.	Questions in multiple thinking strands are consistently relevant to the text with plenty of supporting text evidence.	Questions are generally relevant to the text but are not the *best* questions for the text; they may rely mostly on a couple of thinking strands.	Questions are not a good match for the text and/or focus primarily on a single thinking strand.
The teacher asks higher-level questions that are open ended and elicit divergent responses.	Questions are consistently open ended and promote divergent thinking (even controversy).	There is a mix of literal and higher-level questions.	The questions are almost all literal with a single, right answer.
The teacher uses words and vocabulary that children can understand—but also stretches their thinking.	The academic vocabulary is rich, but the teacher provides sufficient guidance.	The language of some questions makes them hard to understand.	Students are more confused than enlightened by the teacher's use of words.
The teacher models the kinds of discussion behaviors that students should emulate.	The teacher models good discussion behaviors and points these out to students.	The teacher may model but does not explain to students *how* to engage in similar actions.	There is no modeling; the teacher just expects students to figure things out on their own.
The teacher remembers "wait time" in order to encourage student participation.	The teacher always gives students the time to process a question before seeking a response.	Sometimes the teacher uses "wait time" effectively, but other times the pace is too fast.	The teacher calls on the first student to raise his hand.
The teacher does not answer his own question or repeat or paraphrase students' responses.	The teacher knows that faulty questioning strategies will enable, not empower, students.	The teacher sometimes paraphrases students' responses or answers her own questions.	The teacher quickly answers her own question if no student responds or if she gets an incorrect response.
The teacher encourages students to talk to each other, not just to her.	The teacher actively works to get students talking to each other.	The students talk to each other, but most responses come back to the teacher for grounding.	The teacher controls the talk. She poses all of the questions and decides who will talk and when.
The teacher finds strategies to cope with students who try to dominate a discussion.	The teacher (in a kind way) makes sure no student dominates the discussion.	The teacher is aware of domineering students but has trouble dealing with them.	The teacher clearly allows some students to dominate the discussion.
The teacher finds strategies to get reticent children to respond.	The teacher (in a kind way) gets even the quiet children to respond.	The teacher attempts to get quiet students involved, but is often not successful.	The teacher doesn't do anything to get the quiet kids talking—or even engaged.
The teacher attends to her own nonverbal signals and those of her students.	The teacher consistently attends to her nonverbal behaviors and those of her students.	The teacher is aware of the impact of nonverbal cues but does not always attend to them.	The teacher is oblivious to nonverbal cues from her students or herself.
The teacher avoids questions with obvious or one-word answers.	The teacher words questions carefully to avoid "giving away" the answer or allowing students to answer in one word.	Sometimes students can figure out the answer by the order of answer choices, or they can respond with a single word.	Many answers are obvious; there are too many yes/no responses.

DISCUSSION RUBRIC FOR ASSESSING STUDENT DISCOURSE

STUDENT: _____ DATE: _____

	2	1	0
Demonstrates preparation for the discussion	Participation in the discussion demonstrates close reading of the text with many specific text references	Student has clearly read the text, though there are not too many specific details cited	Student does not appear to have read or understood the text; does not refer to specific textual details; references do not make sense
Listens attentively to peers	Shows genuine interest in peers' responses; tracks speaker	Generally focused on response of speaker; sometimes appears distracted or too eager to state own point of view	Does not pay attention to the speaker; off task or too focused on sharing own ideas
Highly engaged; volunteers ideas, but does not dominate discussion	Consistently contributes insightful comments and ideas with good sense of how much talking is appropriate	Sometimes contributes to discussion, but contributions do not show much critical thinking; may try to participate too much	Seldom participates—even when called on by the teacher; very passive or even disruptive
Respects opinions of other group members	Waits until the previous speaker is finished; encourages and supports the opinions of others, even when disagreeing	Generally respectful, but sometimes interrupts speaker or disagrees in a negative way	Interrupts frequently; becomes argumentative when disagreeing
Builds on peers' ideas with comments or further questions	Integrates past comments into own comments; extends ideas by posing additional questions or following up on peers' comments	Sometimes builds on peers' responses with further comments or questions; sometimes changes topic back to own interest	Follow-up comments have nothing to do with preceding conversation; never asks questions
Rethinks opinion based on ideas of other group members	Synthesizes information from multiple sources in order to develop more informed opinion	Sometimes willing to change stance based on input from group members	Emphatically defends own stance—in spite of conflicting evidence

Areas of strength:

_____

Areas of need:

_____

◉ CHECKLIST FOR REFLECTING ON DISCUSSION SKILLS

NAME: _____ **DATE:** _____

Today we had a discussion about: _____

_____

❑   I was prepared for this discussion. I did all the reading and thought about what I might say.

❑   I listened carefully to other people in my group. I looked at them and concentrated on what they were saying.

❑   I joined the discussion without my teacher asking me. I showed that I was interested. I gave other people the chance to talk, too.

❑   I was polite even when I disagreed. I didn't act like my answer was the only good answer.

❑   I connected my response to another speaker's response. I said things like, "My opinion is almost the same as Tim's except…"

❑   I was open minded. I was willing to change my opinion if someone else had a really great idea.

My best moment in this discussion was when: _____

_____

When I am participating in a discussion, I need to get better at:

_____

_____

GUIDELINES AND RESOURCES FOR
A-D STRAND QUESTIONS

Guidelines

These questions are great when you want to provide a general review of the kinds of prompts for open-ended responses that students are likely to see on a state assessment. They are clearly identified within particular strands and standards, so you can make sure you are exposing your students to *all* of the kinds of questions they are likely to encounter on an assessment. There are some questions that teachers tend to omit. Look carefully at the A-D strand questions on pages 106-109. Be honest with yourself: Are there some questions here that you don't ask very often? I'm sure you'll find others, but a few questions that I don't hear very often in classrooms are:

- B1-d: Can this part of the [story/poem] be described as: a description, an explanation, a conversation, an opinion, an argument, or a comparison? How do you know?

- B2-a: Why does the author include paragraph _____?

- D1-e: Do you think the author made this story believable? Why or why not?

Asking A-D strand questions during a general discussion of a text will alert you to objectives that need more review or re-teaching during subsequent small-group sessions.

Resources

- *A-D Strand Questions for Discussion* (questions identified for specific comprehension objectives), pages 106-109 in Chapter Five

- *Discussion Planner for A-D Strand Comprehension Questions* (template for teachers to identify the questions they wish to ask about a text), page 184

- *Rubric for Assessing a Student's Use of Comprehension Strategies* (for teachers to assess students' standards-based comprehension), page 65 in Chapter Four

- *Comprehension Strategy Checklist* (for students to assess their own standards-based comprehension), page 66 in Chapter Four

A. Forming a general understanding

1.

2.

B. Developing an interpretation

1.

2.

C. Connecting and reacting

1.

2.

D. Structure and content

1.

2.

GUIDELINES AND RESOURCES FOR *TALKING STRATEGICALLY ABOUT TEXT*

Guidelines

Another means of discussing text more deeply is to focus the conversation around comprehension strategies. This will serve two purposes. First, it will address students' depth of understanding about the text itself. It will also address their understanding of the reading process, their metacognitive awareness. Questions that relate to comprehension strategies are especially useful for students who just skim the surface as they read. By focusing on what good readers do to achieve more complex knowledge about a text, perhaps they, too, will learn to read more critically. Determine the strategy-based questions you will ask based on the text students have read. Decide which strategies are the most essential to unlocking this text's meaning and begin there with your questions.

Resources

- *Discussion Questions for Deep Thinking about Comprehension Strategies* (to engage in a discussion about text based on metacognitive strategies), pages 186-188

- *Discussion Planner for Comprehension Strategies* (to identify strategy-based questions useful for a particular text), page 189

- *Rubric for Assessing a Student's Use of Comprehension Strategies* (for teachers to assess students' strategy thinking during discussions), page 185 in Chapter Four

- *Comprehension Strategy Checklist* (for students to assess their own strategic thinking during a discussion), page 186 in Chapter Four

DISCUSSION QUESTIONS FOR DEEP THINKING ABOUT COMPREHENSION STRATEGIES

Discussion Questions about Noticing

- **Awareness:** Where did you pause to think about your thinking? Why did you stop at this place (or these places)? What did you think about that helped you understand the story better?

- **Tracking thinking:** *How* did you track your thinking today (sticky notes, margin notes, underlining, something else)? Why did you choose this way of tracking? Is this the way you usually track your thinking? Why?

- **Fix-up strategies:** Was there someplace in your reading today that caused you some confusion? What were you confused about (or what didn't you understand)? Did you get your thinking back on track? How? Or are you still a little confused? Explain!

- **Tuning in to comprehension strategies:** Was there one particular comprehension strategy (wondering, predicting, connecting, figuring out, picturing) that was especially helpful today? Why do you think you used this strategy so much to help you make meaning?

- **Important/not so important:** Today you probably noticed lots of things as you read. Now that you have finished your reading, what really stands out? Choose one or two things you marked in your text and explain why these were so important.

- **Focusing:** Some days it's hard to stay focused on your reading. Was this one of those days for you? Why do you think this happened? What could you do to stay more focused next time?

Discussion Questions about Picturing (Visualizing)

- **Identify snapshots in a text:** Find a passage that you think the author included so we could picture/visualize something in this text. What do you think the author wanted us to understand by including these details?

- **Recall the image:** Using words or pictures, tell about what you see based on details the author provided.

- **Other ways of "seeing":** What other senses help you "see" this passage? What do you taste, hear, smell, feel?

- **Extend the picture:** What *other* details could you add to the picture in your mind that the author didn't include in the text?

- **Words and other author's crafts that help you *see*:** What are the *most* powerful words the author uses to help you picture this [character, setting, etc.]? What other crafts does the author use to help you picture this [character, setting, etc.]?

- **Other ways of seeing:** What is another way of looking at this text? How does that change what you see?

Discussion Questions about Wondering

- **Something is wrong here…:** What was unsettling about what you read today? What questions did that bring to your mind about people's behavior?

- **I'd like to know more about…:** What did you read about today that made you curious to know more? What questions did you wish this book would answer?

- **Titles that grab your attention:** How did the title (or cover) grab your attention? What questions did you have about this book even before reading it?

- **On the edge of my seat:** Where do you think the author *wanted* you to have questions? What part of your reading today was particularly suspenseful?

- **That unfinished feeling:** Sometimes an author "leaves you hanging" and you still have questions when the story ends. What questions remained for you as this story ended? What else do you want to know?

Discussion Questions about Predicting

- **I have a prediction (about this story):** Was there someplace in this story where you were able to make a strong prediction about what would happen next? What was the prediction? What led you to this prediction? Were you right?

- **After the end (of the story):** Imagine that you turned the page after finishing your book and there was one more paragraph (or chapter). What would that paragraph/chapter contain? What would be a probable "next event" in this book?

- **Genre or author clues:** What predictions could you make about this text by knowing the genre or the author?

- **The best clues:** What were the best clues to meaning in the text you read today (either a story or nonfiction)?

- **Pictures and graphics can help:** Which illustration or other graphic gave you the best clues to meaning? What did you predict based on this graphic/illustration?

Discussion Questions about Figuring Out (Inferring)

- **A character learns a lesson:** Who learned an important lesson in this story? What lesson did this character learn? Explain a little about how the character learned this lesson.

- **We learn a lesson from a character:** What can *you* learn from the way this character behaved or acted?

- **The big idea/theme/message/main idea:** What did the author want readers to think about through this text?

- **Another good title:** What would be another good title for this [story]? (Think about the meaning of the story when you choose your new title.)

- **Author's purpose:** Why did the author write this [story] (to entertain, inform, teach a lesson, etc.)?

- **Lifting a line:** Choose a line or a couple of sentences that you feel are important to the text in some way. What is the author trying to *show* with the line or lines? What did the author want you to understand?

- **True for people in general:** Is there a "universal truth" in this story—something that is "true for people in general"? What is it? How did you figure it out?

Discussion Questions about Figuring Out (synthesizing)

- **Put the pieces together:** Paraphrase/summarize/provide the gist of this paragraph/ passage/text.

- **Connect texts:** How does the problem/theme/character/event in "text A" compare to the problem/theme/character/event in "text B"?

- **Merging files:** How does information from "text B" add to what you learned from "text A"?

Discussion Questions about Personal Connections

- **This is *big*!:** Think about the big idea in this book. What is the experience that the author wants you to think about? Has anything like this ever happened to you?

- **I've felt like this…:** What feeling stands out from your reading today? When have you felt this way in your own life?

- **Getting to know you:** Is there anyone in this book you would like to know personally? Why would this person make a good friend?

- **Sounds like fun—or maybe not!:** Would you have enjoyed being part of the experience described in this book? Why or why not?

- **I highly recommend…:** Who do you know who might enjoy this book? Why? What could you say to convince them to read this book themselves?

- **This reminds me of *another* book I read:** Did this book remind you of something else you read? What was the book? What was the connection?

DISCUSSION PLANNER FOR COMPREHENSION STRATEGIES

TITLE OF THE TEXT: _____

Noticing
1.

2.

Picturing
1.

2.

Wondering
1.

2.

Predicting
1.

2.

Figuring out (inferring)
1.

2.

Figuring out (synthesizing)
1.

2.

Making personal connections
1.

2.

GUIDELINES AND RESOURCES FOR *THINKING OUTSIDE THE BOX*

Guidelines

Both teachers and students love these "box" icons. Anything that can be depicted with a symbol—something concrete—is helpful for categorizing our thinking. (Contrast this to Bloom's Taxonomy which, although very systematic, is challenging for teachers to really grasp—and almost impossible for students to conceptualize.) Teachers "get" these boxes quickly and easily create "box" questions for a given text. After responding to "box" questions for a while, students can invent suitable questions, too. It is not necessary to have a question for every box. Focus on questions that will likely generate the most discussion. I introduce the boxes (ways of thinking about a text) beforehand using the mini-posters ("Thinking Outside the Box Mini-Posters" on the CD) to give students an initial understanding of the concept. That is usually all that is needed. Note that all of these templates are in color on the CD to make them even more engaging.

Resources

- *Thinking Outside the Box Template* (for teachers or students to identify questions for different ways of thinking about a text), page 192

- *Thinking Outside the Box Template with Suggested Generic Questions* (note that these are only *suggested* questions; other questions can certainly be identified for each thinking box), page 191

- *Thinking Outside the Box Mini-Posters* (I duplicate these double-sided with the large box icons on one side and the generic questions on the reverse), "Thinking Outside the Box Mini-Posters" on the CD

- *Critical-thinking Rubric* (for teachers to evaluate students' critical thinking), page 193

- *Critical-thinking Checklist* (for students to evaluate their own critical thinking), page 194

Plain Cardboard Box	**BASIC THINKING** Summarize what you read. What do you know about each character? Tell the events in order. What strategies did you use to keep your thinking on track? What was the problem and how was it solved?
Juice Box	**JUICY DETAILS** What details could you really picture in your mind? What were some of the best words Which details were the most interesting? Why did the author include _____?
Heart Box	**FEELINGS** Was there a character in this story that you cared about a lot? Why? Is there anything from this text you will keep in your heart for a long time? How did the author get you to like some characters and dislike others? What was your first reaction when...?
Unusual Box	**CREATIVE THINKING** Did anyone in this story think creatively to solve a problem? How would this story have been different if it took place in another time or place? In what ways did the author demonstrate creativity in writing this story? What if...? If this story became a movie, who would you choose to play the part of _____? What might happen next if the author added another page/chapter?
Broken Box FRAGILE	**PROBLEMS AND ISSUES** Did anyone in this story make a bad decision? Explain. What would *you* have done if you were _____? Did any of the characters demonstrate a negative character trait? Explain. Were there any unfortunate outcomes of a character's actions? What were they? Did anyone learn a hard lesson? Did anyone take a big risk? Explain.
Treasure Box	**SOMETHING TO TREASURE** What did you like best? What were the *best* lines? Do you consider any of these characters to be a real "gem?" Why? What "nuggets" will you take from this text? Was there anything about this story that spoke directly to *you*?

THINKING OUTSIDE THE BOX

Plain Cardboard Box	**BASIC THINKING**
Juice Box	**JUICY DETAILS**
Heart Box	**FEELINGS**
Unusual Box	**CREATIVE THINKING**
Broken Box	**PROBLEMS AND ISSUES**
Treasure Box	**SOMETHING TO TREASURE**

CRITICAL-THINKING RUBRIC

STUDENT: _____ DATE: _____

	2 Exemplary	1 Satisfactory	0 Unsatisfactory
Problem/question /issue	Clearly articulates the essential problem, question, or issue; sees beneath the surface	Identifies the core problem, question, or issue, but perception lacks depth	Does not recognize the core problem, question, or issue or only sees superficial elements
Openness	Willingly examines multiple points of view with fair-mindedness and empathy	Recognizes and listens to opposing points of view	Cannot get past her/his own point of view when examining an issue
Key concepts	Identifies all of the key concepts and big ideas	Identified concepts are a mix of key ideas and smaller details	Unable to identify key concepts or sees no distinction between main concepts and small details
Elaboration	Provides full elaboration of key concepts with the most useful details	Provides adequate elaboration, but could be more specific in some cases	Elaboration is inadequate; too general
Inferences	Makes deep, relevant inferences	Inferences are relevant but lack depth of thinking	Is not able to infer, or inferences are irrelevant
Implications	Recognizes probable from improbable implications; predicts consequences based on solid inferential thinking	Sees probable implications, but doesn't elaborate on predictions using solid inferences	Does not recognize the likely outcome of a situation; predictions are not based on reasonable inferences

Critical-thinking strengths: _____

_____

Critical-thinking needs: _____

_____

NAME: _____ **DATE:** _____

1. _____ I was able to clearly identify the **problem, issue, or concern**, not just the surface-level problem, but the problem below the surface.

2. _____ I was **open** to other people's views and showed that I really cared about opinions other than my own.

3. _____ I recognized all of the **main points** related to this problem or issue.

4. _____ I was able to **elaborate** on all of the main points by providing evidence from the text.

5. _____ I made **inferences** from the text that showed great reasoning.

6. _____ I saw the **consequences** or **implications** of this problem (what would likely occur in the future) because of the way this situation was handled or resolved.

The best thing about my critical thinking today was

_____

_____

I would like to grow in critical thinking by

_____

_____

GUIDELINES AND RESOURCES FOR
FACING FACTS: QUESTIONS FOR INFORMATIONAL TEXT

Guidelines

Although you can (and should) use the A-D strand questions for informational text, and other protocols for questioning in this chapter will also work pretty well for this purpose, it is the questions that follow that will generate the deepest thinking about informational text. Note that I have used the label *informational text* rather than *nonfiction* because it is more inclusive. *Many* kinds of text give us information, including historical fiction and narrative nonfiction—text that provides information (frequently about an animal) by turning the basic facts into a story in order to make it more interesting and memorable. Information does not need to be presented in an expository format (main ideas and details, the way most social studies and science texts are organized). For example, a biography is informational, but it is narrative, not expository.

I have classified these questions for informational text using the 2009 NAEP (National Assessment of Educational Progress) framework because NAEP is so heavily weighted in favor of informational text and uses so many informational formats for assessing students' thinking. NAEP thinking categories include: Locate and Recall; Integrate and Interpret; and Critique and Evaluate. I did, however, add a category, Extend and Apply, because I believe it is important to also address students' potential use of information in real-world situations.

As with other questioning protocols, feel free to focus on just a few questions that seem best suited to today's text. And, of course, choose your text carefully to make sure students have enough background knowledge to bring to what they read, as well as a stake in what happens in their world because of this information.

Resources

- *Facing Facts: Questions for Informational Text* (to be used by the teacher—and possibly students, too—to devise great discussion questions for informational text), page 196

- *Discussion Planner for Informational Text* (to plan questions for a particular informational text), page 197

- *Rubric for Comprehending Informational Text* (for the teacher to assess students' thinking about informational text), page 198

- *Checklist for Comprehending Informational Text* (for students to assess their own thinking about informational text), page 199

FACING FACTS: QUESTIONS FOR INFORMATIONAL TEXT

LOCATE AND RECALL

- Can you identify the facts? The opinions?
- What kind of research do you think the author had to do to write this book?
- What words or sentences does the author use that caught your attention? Why?
- What words stood out to you as absolutely essential to understanding this information?
- If you could ask only three questions about this information to test a reader's basic understanding, what do you think would be the most important questions to ask?
-

INTEGRATE AND INTERPRET

- Were there any photographs, illustrations, charts, graphs, or diagrams that you thought were important? Select one, show what you learned from it, and explain why you believe it was important.
- Was there anything in the way this text was written or presented that made it easy or difficult to understand? Explain.
- What is the author's point of view about this topic? How can you tell?

CRITIQUE AND EVALUATE

- What information from this text seems most important to share with someone else? Why?
- Does the author try to persuade you in any way? How?
- Do you find the author's evidence convincing? Explain.
- How did this new information change your way of thinking about this subject?
- How did you connect to the piece? Was it personal? Was it an issue that affects your community? The world? Explain.
- Is there any information here that you question or think might not be correct? Explain.
- What is the most interesting thing you read?
- Would this be a useful/interesting text for older readers? Younger readers?

EXTEND AND APPLY

- What else would you like to learn about this topic?
- How can you apply this information to an issue or problem in today's world?
- What questions would you ask the author if you had the chance to meet him or her?
- Did the reading leave you with unanswered questions? What are they?
- Where could you look for more information on this topic?
- Would you like to read more books on this topic? Why or why not?
- Who would benefit from reading this book/article?

LOCATE AND RECALL

1.

2.

INTEGRATE AND INTERPRET

1.

2.

CRITIQUE AND EVALUATE

1.

2.

EXTEND AND APPLY

1.

2.

RUBRIC FOR COMPREHENDING INFORMATIONAL TEXT

NAME: _____ DATE: _____

TEXT: _____

	2 Outstanding	1 Good progress	0 Needs work
Use of text features	Routinely uses multiple text features to find and understand information	Understands text features but uses them inconsistently to achieve understanding	Does not seem to understand or use text features as keys to meaning
Use of text structures	Easily recognizes many text structures (main idea/ details, cause/ effect, compare/ contrast, etc.) to aid comprehension	Recognizes basic text structures (main idea/ details, sequence) and uses structures to aid comprehension	Does not seem to grasp the concept of text structure; unable to use structure as an aid to comprehension
Understanding of important ideas and details	Clearly understands important ideas and details as demonstrated by summarizing, inferring, and synthesizing	Understands ideas and details when they are not too complex or when they do not require too much inference	Often misses key ideas and details in a text; unable to summarize
Recognition that author's use of language and style contribute to meaning	Easily identifies elements of the author's craft that contribute to meaning or enjoyment of a text	Recognizes powerful words and phrases but less adept at recognizing other elements of style	Does not seem to have any understanding of how language and style can impact meaning
Recognition of the author's purpose and perspective in contributing to meaning	Clearly recognizes the author's viewpoint and considers this when drawing personal conclusions about a text	Recognizes the author's viewpoint but does not reflect critically on this when drawing conclusions about a text	Does not seem to understand the concept of author's purpose or perspective
Connection and application of text content to real-world situations	Readily recognizes real-world connections to text information and may even propose "action" step	Makes real-world connections with a bit of guidance	Appears to have no personal interest in any possible real-world text connection

Best feature of informational text comprehension: _____

_____

Something to work on: _____

_____

CHECKLIST FOR COMPREHENDING INFORMATIONAL TEXT

NAME: _____ **DATE:** _____

_____ I used informational **text features** (like illustrations, captions, and boldfaced words) to help me understand this text.

_____ I used **text structures** (like main idea/details, sequence, cause/effect, compare/contrast) to help me understand this text.

_____ I showed that I understood this informational text because I could **summarize** it and make good **inferences**.

_____ I could explain how the author's language and style of writing contributed to the meaning of the text.

_____ I could figure out the author's purpose or perspective and how this contributed to the text's message.

_____ I could make connections between what I read and a situation or something else in our world today.

Something I'm proud of today: _____

_____

_____

Something I'd like to improve on: _____

_____

_____

GUIDELINES AND RESOURCES FOR *CHANGE IT UP: QUESTIONS AND TASKS FOR CREATIVE THINKING*

Guidelines

Our current world of education is not one that celebrates creativity. As we are reminded daily, accountability rules! *Creative thinking* and *data collection* rarely find themselves in the same sentence and, as a result, we have drifted further and further from offering students the kinds of experiences that challenge them not just to analyze and evaluate text (critical thinking), but to actually *do* something based on what they read. How can they *use* what they have learned from a text to extend, apply, or take action? I taught for a few years in a program for gifted students and couldn't help noticing that all the best creative-thinking resources were located within the gifted program curriculum. *All* kids need opportunities for creative thinking. Yes, really bright children thrive on creativity—another way for them to exercise their fine minds. But these quirky, nontraditional applications of text are exactly what some of our less stellar and less motivated students need to engage more passionately in literacy.

Change It Up: Questions and Tasks for Creative Thinking encourages students to manipulate text in ways that tap components of thinking creatively: fluency, flexibility, originality, and elaboration. To achieve a reasonable compromise with the "accountability factor," I have incorporated a product associated with each thinking task (in addition to the discussion that can precede it). I have also provided a rubric and checklist for assessment purposes. While some subjectivity will certainly be inherent in evaluating students' creative products, this is at least a place to begin.

Resources

- *Change It Up: Questions and Tasks for Creative Thinking* (challenge students' creative thinking about text with one or more of these creative-thinking topics), page 201

- *Unlikely Connections: Icons to Symbolize Our Thinking* (use these icons or "real objects" to make a creative connection between text and real life), page 202

- *Creative-thinking Rubric* (for teachers to use to assess students' creative thinking), page 203

- *Creative-thinking Checklist* (for students to use to assess their own creative thinking), page 204

CHANGE IT UP: QUESTIONS AND TASKS FOR CREATIVE THINKING

Write about it can include formats such as plays, poems, and songs as well as traditional narratives.

	Think about it...Talk about it...	Write about it...*
Change the setting	• What if this story occurred somewhere else or in a different time? • Where would you set this story? Why? • How would the story change?	Rewrite a portion of this story with a different setting. This could mean a different time, a different place, or both a different time and place.
Add a character	• What character from a different story, famous person from history, or individual from our world today would make an interesting addition to this story? • How would this character's or person's point of view, skills, or traits be useful to resolving the problem in this story? • How might the story change?	Rewrite a portion of this story, adding in your new character or person. Be sure to show how this individual changes events in the story.
After the end	• If there was a chapter or page after the final chapter or page of your book, what might happen next? • Would the story feel more "finished?" • Would another adventure begin? • Would the characters show they learned a lesson?	Write what happens next—after the story ends. Consider what you know about the characters, their problems, and the way the story ended. Your next page or next chapter should show how well you understand the story's characters and events.
Special power	• What if the main character in this story (or another character) had a special power or skill that could "save the day?" • What would this talent be? Would it be magical? • How would story events change?	Rewrite a portion of this story giving one of the characters a special talent or skill. Show how this special talent or skill changes events in the story.
New narrator	• How would this story be different if it was told from the point of view of a different narrator? • Who else could tell this story? This would probably mean telling the story from the perspective of another character/person in the text. Or it could mean telling the story from the point of view of a *thing*. Find a significant object in the book (a hat, a pen, a horse) and think about how the events would look from this thing's perspective.	Rewrite a portion of this story, giving it a different narrator—perhaps one of the characters or a thing or object in the story. Events in the story should be interpreted differently based on this different point of view.
Different decision	• What if a character in this story had made just one decision different from the choice s/he actually made? • How would this different decision have changed the story from that point on?	Rewrite a portion of this story with one of the characters making a decision different from the one that was actually made. Show how this decision changed what happened next.
Unlikely connections	• Choose an icon (see *Unlikely Connections* sheet) that you think represents some aspect of this text. (It could be a character, the problem, etc.). • How is this icon connected to this text? • What does it symbolize?	Build a solid argument to explain why your icon is a good symbol to represent this text. Go for the less obvious, the connection that no one else might recognize.

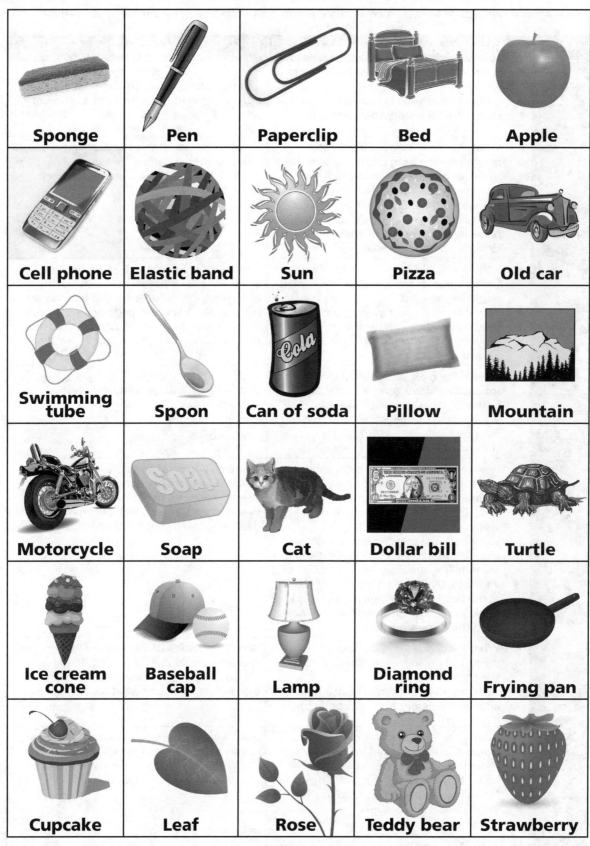

Sponge	Pen	Paperclip	Bed	Apple
Cell phone	Elastic band	Sun	Pizza	Old car
Swimming tube	Spoon	Can of soda	Pillow	Mountain
Motorcycle	Soap	Cat	Dollar bill	Turtle
Ice cream cone	Baseball cap	Lamp	Diamond ring	Frying pan
Cupcake	Leaf	Rose	Teddy bear	Strawberry

 **CREATIVE-THINKING RUBRIC**

NAME: _____ DATE: _____

TEXT: _____

TASK: _____

	2	**1**	**0**
Fluency	The thinking is characterized by *many* details, ideas, or examples—more than would be expected in a given situation	The thinking is characterized by a sufficient number of supportive ideas, examples, or details	The thinking lacks evidence of a sufficient number of supportive ideas, examples, or details
Flexibility	Thoughtfully considers many possibilities and approaches before moving forward with an idea	Recognizes a couple of different approaches before moving forward with an idea	Moves forward with an idea before considering other possibilities
Originality	The perspective is truly unique, clever, and unusual	The perspective is somewhat interesting, though not really unique or original	The thinking is reasonable but doesn't offer a unique or original perspective, or the ideas are unique but implausible
Elaboration	The thinking is well developed with thorough expansion of each idea through carefully articulated details	The thinking is uneven with some ideas fully expanded, while others are a bit too general	The thinking is not developed in a way that incorporates specific details

Comments: _____

_____

_____

_____

_____

CREATIVE-THINKING CHECKLIST

NAME: _____ **DATE:** _____

TEXT: _____

TASK: _____

_____ My thinking shows **fluency**. (I have a lot of ideas represented in the product I produced to go along with this task.)

_____ My thinking shows **flexibility**. (I considered many different options before moving ahead with my task and approached it from different perspectives.)

_____ My thinking shows **originality**. (I don't think many other people would have approached this task the way I did or produced a product like mine.)

_____ My thinking shows **elaboration**. (I developed my ideas fully with lots of thoughtful details, examples, and other kinds of evidence.)

Here's what I like best about the way I completed this creative-thinking task:

_____

_____

Here's what I want to work on to improve my creative thinking:

_____

_____

Chapter Seven

When They "Can't Read"—Teaching Primary Skills in the Intermediate Grades

OH, NO!

It's panic time for some intermediate-grade teachers when they see on their class roster for the coming year that there are students who "can't read." Now "can't read" may be a bit of an exaggeration. What this probably means is that there is a student (or a group of students) reading significantly below grade level with fluency somewhere within the first- to second-grade range.

"I have no idea how to teach beginning reading," these teachers wail. With the advent of RTI (Response to Intervention) this becomes an even greater dilemma because the classroom teacher is now expected to provide that critical first tier of instruction to *all* children in her class—even the really low-performing ones who may previously have been whisked away by the reading specialist for their small-group instruction.

The fallback plan too frequently is to search out a leveled book matched to these readers' instructional level and "do guided reading." In the first chapter of this book, I proposed that a traditional guided reading format wasn't appropriate for intermediate-grade students when the essential need was comprehension. Now I need to amend that to suggest that traditional guided reading will also be ineffective in the intermediate grades when the need is developing primary-level literacy competencies.

DEVELOPING FUNDAMENTAL LITERACY COMPETENCIES

What are those fundamental literacy competencies and why isn't guided reading sufficient? The short answer to the competency question is that beginning readers must learn to integrate all of the components of fluent reading. Fluency doesn't ensure comprehension—but it is difficult to comprehend without fluency. Unlike the fluency focus in Chapter Five: Reinforcing Skills and Strategies, where the emphasis was on prosody (reading with feeling) as a component of comprehension, the focus for students in the intermediate grades who continue to struggle with getting to fluency must be on automaticity—recognizing words automatically without needing to concentrate on decoding. But even this isn't enough. The outcome must be accurate reading of connected text at an appropriate rate—which then sets the stage for prosody.

Traditional guided reading provides opportunities for students to *practice* their reading in leveled text under the watchful eye of their teacher who guides their use of strategies: "Does this sound right? Does it look right? Does it make sense?" But it doesn't offer systematic attention to the skills that allow children to discern "Does it look right?" That is, there is no defined curriculum in word recognition. And that *must* be a component of small-group instruction for students still striving to achieve basic fluency. Efficient word recognition requires attention to two things, neither of which guarantees fluency, though they do support it: instruction in decoding (phonics) and instruction in sight words.

Some proponents of guided reading view the time teachers spend with students in small groups as a "session" rather than a "lesson." The message here is that the focus is on *practice* rather than *instruction*. Practice is definitely not enough for students in the intermediate grades who are reading far below grade-level expectancy. Let's be clear that we need to *instruct* these children in their small groups. The difference, however, between instruction for these students and instruction for their peers close to, on, or above grade level is that rather than *one* specific lesson focus, you will now need to integrate four different components into each lesson: sight words, decoding, comprehension, and fluency.

The classroom teacher's most important goal with intermediate-grade students reading significantly below grade level is to get them "unstuck" and moving forward; it is not to pass the state test. If that is your only measure of success, both you and your striving students will quickly conclude that this is a failed mission. (You cannot—in most cases—make up three or four years of literacy deficits in a single year.) Instead, know where you are starting—not just the reading level, but the skills that are in place and those that comprise the critical next step. Then, get a plan: Where can you realistically (but ambitiously with high expectations) hope these students will be by the end of the year? Now set that plan in motion so you actually reach that goal. We can't magically close the achievement gap overnight. But we can close it over time if we all work together to make that happen.

QUESTIONS TO CONSIDER

1. What seems to be the biggest challenge for your struggling students?

2. Why do you think these students continue to struggle with basic reading skills beyond the primary grades?

3. What seems to work with these students? What doesn't work?

4. What kind of support would be most helpful to you in order to support your struggling students?

5. What questions do you hope the remainder of this chapter will answer for you?

INSTRUCTIONAL FOCUS: PRIMARY READING

What's the purpose?

The purpose is to integrate multiple components of reading into a single lesson (sight words, decoding, fluency, vocabulary/comprehension) in such a way that intermediate-grade students stuck at the primary level can move toward grade-level reading performance.

Who would benefit from this focus?

This approach works best for students in the intermediate grades experiencing significant delays in reading who have not previously been exposed to a consistently implemented comprehensive instructional approach. "Comprehensive," in this regard, means incorporating systematic phonics instruction and an emphasis on sight words along with comprehension and fluency. If students *have* had this kind of explicit instruction in the past and it has not worked, the issue might be something deeper than lack of explicit teaching. In that case, further assessment will be needed with follow-up Tier 2 or even Tier 3 targeted interventions.

What kinds of texts should I use?

The obvious answer to this question is to use text at an appropriate instructional level such as those small guided reading books. Remember, though, when you select your texts, that these are big(ger) kids who will be reading them. They are not going to be excited by content that is obviously more juvenile than they are (for example, a story about losing your first tooth). They will not want to see illustrations that feature little children playing in a sandbox. They need to learn the rudiments of reading—with their dignity and pride intact. Consider using short plays. Not only do you get to legitimately read the content again and again as you practice for "performance," but plays are interactive and get all of your kids involved in a positive way. Nonfiction is often a good option for below-level readers, too, since the content tends to be less age specific. And don't forget about poetry. Poems are short and don't overwhelm readers with pages and pages to read (cause for panic when you're worried about whether you can even get through the first sentence). The natural rhythm of poetry also lends itself to more fluent oral reading.

What resources will I need for teaching and assessing?

- *Small-group Planner for Levels 18-20 and Below* (for planning your instruction over three days), page 211

- *Sample Three-day Plan for Levels 18-20 and Below* (to use as a model for creating your own plan), page 210

- *Rubric for Assessing Students' Integration of Foundational Reading Skills* (for the teacher to assess students), page 212

- *Reading Skills Checklist* (for students' self-reflection), page 213

How do I implement this?

On any given day, the proportion of time devoted to each area may vary, but the following general principles can guide your work. (For more detail about the content of each component for readers at different levels, see the chart in Chapter Two: *Differentiated Small-group Instruction: Integrating All Components of Fluent Reading* on pages 17-25.)

1. Five minutes of sight words instruction (Dolch list or another list of high-frequency words; not words specific to a particular text). This could consist of flash cards or a simple game—though my preference is to keep the pace quick and minimize the game playing.

2. Five minutes of decoding instruction (systematic and explicit based on a continuum of skills). This could include word sorts or other activities aligned with phonic skill level.

3. Ten minutes of comprehension/fluency instruction, including, but not limited to: book introduction; vocabulary; "whisper reading" or oral reading for accuracy, rate, and expression; follow-up questions (both literal and inferential).

Although the planning template on page 210 suggests three days per book, two days or even a single day may be sufficient for a particular text. As books become longer and more complex, more than one day may be needed to complete an initial reading—one day for the first half of the text and a second day for the second half. Other variations could be possible, too.

Consider making the following guided reading adjustments to your small-group instruction for students reading at an early primary level:

- Limit the use of picture walks when the illustrations give away too much about the plot of the story or when students would benefit more from looking at a selected illustration or two to pique their curiosity or help them make useful predictions.

- Limit the use of whisper reading. Oral reading fluency can be monitored by asking students to identify evidence that proves a particular point. ("Read the sentence on page 4 that explains why the character was upset when…")

- Introduce content vocabulary page by page rather than introducing all new words before reading. This facilitates more immediate transfer.

- Set page-by-page goals (unless there are just a couple of words per page) and ask students to read individual pages with the specific purpose in mind. This will reinforce the concept of retrieving necessary evidence. As readers become more competent, extend the purpose over two pages or three.

How do I measure students' success?

Since the purpose of this instructional focus is to "fill in the gaps" for students and move their reading performance closer to grade level, "closing in on grade-level performance" needs to be the main criteria in measuring success:

- **Level 1:** Showing improvement, but improvement is slow; still performing significantly below grade level

- **Level 2:** Showing good improvement; will probably make more than one year's growth in a year to move closer to grade level

- **Level 3:** Showing rapid improvement; will soon catch up to on-level peers

SAMPLE THREE-DAY PLAN FOR LEVELS 18-20 AND BELOW

Day	Instructional focus	Objective to review, model, and practice during small group	Follow-up task to be completed before next small group
Day 1	**Sight words**	Introduce 1-3 new words; review about 20 words (based on students' level)	**Possible tasks:** • Create sight word sentences/phrases • Phonics follow-up sorting actvity • Partner read for fluency practice • Respond to comprehension question in complete written sentence • Independent reading • Journal writing • Oral language activity
	Decoding	Review/extend phonics (or PA) concept based on systematic progression	
	Comprehension/ vocabulary	Introduce book including 1-2 content words follow-up questions to check text elements/big ideas	
	Fluency	All students whisper-read book with teacher monitoring for accuracy, rate, expression, phrasing (as appropriate), OR Students read orally to verify evidence in the text	
Day 2	**Sight words**	Introduce 1-3 new words; review about 20 words (based on students' level)	**Possible tasks:** • See above
	Decoding	Review/extend phonics (or PA) concept based on systematic progression	
	Comprehension/ vocabulary	Review book; focus on specific comprehension objective	
	Fluency	May whisper-read text again to build fluency or reread portions, orally focusing on accuracy, rate, expression, phrasing	
Day 3	**Sight words**	Introduce 1-3 new words; review about 20 words (based on students' level)	**Possible tasks:** • See above
	Decoding	Review/extend phonics (or PA) concept based on systematic progression	
	Comprehension/ vocabulary	Ask one or two higher-level comprehension questions, focusing on the art of discourse	
	Fluency	Reread portions of the text orally focusing on accuracy, rate, expression, phrasing	

NAME: _____ DATE: _____

Day	Instructional focus	Objective to review, model, and practice during small group	Follow-up task to be completed before next small group
Day 1	Sight words		
	Decoding		
	Comprehension/vocabulary	Text: _____	
	Fluency		
Day 2	Sight words		
	Decoding		
	Comprehension/vocabulary	Text: _____	
	Fluency		
Day 3	Sight words		
	Decoding		
	Comprehension/vocabulary	Text: _____	
	Fluency		

RUBRIC FOR ASSESSING STUDENTS' INTEGRATION OF FOUNDATIONAL READING SKILLS

STUDENT'S NAME: _____ GRADE: _____ DATE: _____

	Excellent = 2	Developing = 1	Needs attention = 0
Progress with retention and use of sight words	Excellent progress learning and retaining new sight words; quick recall; applies sight words while reading	Seems to learn new words relatively easily but doesn't always retain them and sometimes doesn't recognize them in context	Difficulty learning new words and remembering them; often does not recognize sight words while reading
Progress with decoding	Applies learned phonics concepts to accurately segment and blend sounds	Identifies sounds made by individual letters and letter patterns, but has difficulty blending and segmenting them	Difficulty identifying sounds made by individual letters and letter patterns; much difficulty with segmenting and blending
Progress with fluency	Applies sight words and decoding skills in order to read accurately at a reasonable rate	Sight words and decoding skills appear adequate, but reading is not smooth	Poor decoding skills and low sight-word knowledge make reading dysfluent
Progress with comprehension (basic construction of meaning)	Looks for text elements and applies comprehension strategies *during* reading; Accurately retells story after reading it in order to validate comprehension	Although reading is fluent and comprehension strategies are applied during reading, after-reading comprehension checks sometimes lack specifics	Lack of decoding skills, sight-word knowledge, and fluency make even basic comprehension difficult

Strengths: _____

_____

_____

Needs: _____

_____

_____

NAME: _____ **DATE:** _____

1. _____ I am doing a good job learning and remembering new sight words, and I know them when I am reading, too.

2. _____ I know the sounds of letters and groups of letters, and I can put them together to figure out a word I don't recognize.

3. _____ When I read out loud, my reading sounds smooth, just like talking. I get the words right.

4. _____ After I read, I can retell the story or the information with plenty of details.

I can tell that my reading is improving by the way I

_____

_____

_____

One way I would like to improve my reading is to

_____

_____

_____

Afterword

I trust you now have plenty of ideas for your intermediate-grade small-group instruction—and the skills to deliver that instruction with passion and power. Return now to those classroom scenarios on pages 3-7 and the *Three-day Small-group Reading Plan* on page 30 in Chapter Two. Rethink what you might insert in the "Focus" column for each day. Do you have some thoughts about which instructional formats would work best with a particular group on Day 1? Day 2? Day 3? Then I'd say you've learned your lesson well.

If you can envision the instructional possibilities for a hypothetical group of students, you can do the same for your own students. Helping you imagine those possibilities was the reason I felt compelled to write this book. I believe I have accomplished that goal. The next step belongs to you.

No one but you can write your actual small-group lessons as you'll need to think about what went well or not so well today to move forward with the best agenda for tomorrow. You need to not only recognize and understand the possibilities; you need to devise a means for setting that plan in motion. I have every confidence that you're up to that challenge.

Notes

Notes